TO HELL AND BACK
THE LIFE STORY OF AN AUSTRIAN WORLD WAR II SURVIVOR

Copyright © 2014 by Maria Rosa

All rights reserved.

Without limiting the rights under copyright reserved above, no part of this publication may be reproduced, distributed, transmitted, stored in or introduced into a retrieval system, in any form or by any means, including photocopying, recording, or other electronic or mechanical methods, or otherwise, without the prior written permission of the publisher and copyright owner of this book, except in the case of brief quotations embodied in critical reviews and certain other noncommercial uses permitted by copyright law.

In accordance with the U.S. Copyright Act of 1976, the scanning, uploading, and distribution of this book via the Internet or via any other means without the written permission of the publisher and copyright owner is illegal piracy and theft of the author's intellectual property, and is punishable by law.

Please purchase only authorized editions, and do not participate in or encourage electronic piracy of copyrighted materials. Your support of the author's rights is appreciated.

The publisher and copyright holder are not responsible for websites (or their content) that are not owned by the publisher and copyright holder.

First Edition Paperback

First Printing, 2014

ISBN 978-0-9960359-1-0

TO HELL AND BACK
*THE LIFE STORY OF AN AUSTRIAN
WORLD WAR II SURVIVOR*

by
Maria Rosa

Maria Rosa

Publisher's Note

To Hell and Back: The Life Story of an Austrian World War II Survivor is available in hardcover (hardbound), softcover (trade paperback), and Kindle (digital ebook) formats. The ebook features color photographs, vintage postcards, and extras not included in the printed editions.

Available from Amazon.com, CreateSpace.com, and other retail outlets. To order any of these various editions, please visit Amazon.com or other online book stores and search by title or author. The collectible First Edition Hardcover is also available through Lulu.com.

Table of Contents

Part One: Childhood in Austria 8
- BEGINNINGS 9
- THE "JEWISH LETTERS" 12
- LOVE BETWEEN JEWS AND GENTILES 16
- CLOSE CALLS WITH MY BROTHER 19
- HOLY SMOKE 23
- THE SANCTUARY 25
- FOR THE BIRDS 28
- YELLOW ARMBANDS IN VIENNA 31
- THE NAZI TAKEOVER 34
- MORTAR STRUDEL 36
- NAZI ENCOUNTERS 38
- IDENTIFIED FLYING OBJECTS 42
- REFUGEES OF WAR 44
- ABANDONED IN THE ALPS 46
- PEDALING FOR LIFE 48
- VICTORY DAY 49
- THE STAINLESS STEEL POT 52
- THE KAISER'S BRIDGE 54
- SHIFTING SANDS 57
- SCHOOL FIASCOS 60
- A HUNGER GAME 65

Part Two: Seeing the World 67
- ROYAL PAINS IN LONDON 68
- THE BEEFEATERS 72
- CHURCHILL'S ISLAND 76

JUBILEE	79
RITES OF PASSAGE	84
MR. SEWERMEISTER	94
SATURNIA: VOMIT ON THE HIGH SEAS	98

Part Three: Adventures in Canada and Abroad 101

THE END OF THE WORLD	102
PEACHES AND ICE	104
THE ONTARIO QUINTUPLETS	106
WHERE'S THE BEEF?	109
CAT'S SOUP	111
THE FREEMASON'S SHRINE	113
THE MAYOR'S TOUR	116
MY FIRST LOVE	122
A SLAP IN THE FACE	125
DANCING ON THIN ICE	129
MY STALKER	134
THRICE ENSLAVED	136
SOMETHING SMELLS FISHY	139
PENNY CRIMES	141
CHAINED TO WEDLOCK	144
A LABOR OF LOVE	146
ON HANDS AND KNEES	148
MOTHERLY INSTINCTS	150
DISLOCATION	154
CALIFORNIA DREAMING	157

Part Four: American Dreams 159

THE ROADTRIP FROM HELL	160
DESERTED IN HOLLYWOOD	163
EMERGENCY CALLS	165

An Unwelcome Visitor 167
The Cuban Missile Crisis 170
The Assassination of JFK 172
His *Other* Other Family 175
Open For Business 178
The Moon Landing 180
Freedom from Oppression 182
The Sylmar Earthquake 184
The Longest War 187
Energy Crisis 191

Part Five: Global Connections 195
Life and Death 196
Betrayal 200
Insult to Injury 204
Aussie Adventures 207
A Square Meal 210
Bushwalk 216
Mozart's Birthplace 222
Eagle's Nest 228
The Dungeon 234
Cathedral of the Saints 241
Gypsy Music and Garden Gnomes 245
The Truffles of Venus 251
The Ronald Reagan Presidential Library 255
The Northridge Earthquake 261
Sour Melodies 267
Life's Lessons 271

Maria Rosa

Part One: Childhood in Austria

Figure 1. Nazi March.

Beginnings

My mother was 18 years old, and my father 22 when I was born. My earliest recollection reaches back to the age of four, when I was living in a small town in Styria, Austria. I have many fond memories of my good times there as a small child.

The area was surrounded by old medieval castles, and I remember visiting about four of them. The nearby landscape also featured many wide open fields, green meadows, luscious trees, and scenic rivers, where I often frolicked about in playful exploration. We went swimming many times, and the water was as clear as crystal. The early years of my childhood were marked by joy, freedom, and a close-knit community of family and friends who all cared for one another.

I was born in 1932, which makes me 82 years old now. In 1938, Hitler's Nazi forces occupied Austria and annexed the country into the German *Reich*, during the event known as the *Anschluss*. With the *Anschluss*, the German-speaking Republic of Austria ceased to exist as an independent state. Many opposed this move, but the Austrian people were given no choice in the matter. It was not until 1955 that Austria would again regain full sovereignty.

All of my fun and good times with my family came to an abrupt halt when the war began in 1939, after the Nazi German invasion of Poland. I was about 7 years old and had already eagerly attended first grade in elementary school, which I completed with good marks.

By 1939, the consequences of Hitler's takeover were reverberating throughout every area of life. Our school system also changed dramatically. We lost many of our old teachers; new teachers came in that were unfamiliar to us. The standard greeting amongst the schoolchildren and townspeople, "Grüß Gott" ("God greets (you)") was replaced with "Heil Hitler!" ("Hail Hitler!"). This was greatly resented by many Austrians, especially the old-timers.

I had already learned to write in the first grade, but our writing was also reformed. We students had to start all over again with a different alphabet and a different way of writing - which I'll explain later on.

In the meantime, my father was drafted into the German armed services in spite of having a heart condition. My family moved to a different town in order to be close to my grandmother. We all started to live in her house, as times grew more and more difficult for us.

Now, during the period when I went to school, there were no school busses. There was not even a school in town; so every morning I had to climb up the mountain to reach a different township, where there was a huge castle with an outlying church, and a schoolhouse. It was a small farming community, and quite an idyllic place, but the daily trek was long and arduous. Going to school was therefore very exhausting, and coming back home during the winter when it was snowing, even more so.

I attended elementary school until the age of 10, which was in 1942. I then switched over to secondary school, after my family moved to yet another small town. There was no school or public transportation in this community either, so we children had to ride our bicycles to get to secondary school, whether winter or summer, snow or rain.

By 1942 the Second World War was in full swing, and we children were very afraid, and always hungry and cold. Food was terribly scarce; anything like butter, eggs, or milk was almost impossible to obtain – unless you had a connection with a farmer and bartered whatever you had in exchange, starting from your jewelry, to your clothes, to your shoes. The Nazi-issued rations we got later were extremely meager, and you couldn't just help yourself to the available food: rations queues at the market were so long that you would often line up for six hours before someone would help you.

Trying to get an education was extremely difficult during these years, as we spent half of our time in cold cellars, scared out of our skulls that we would get bombed again - which happened several times. Grandmother's house practically crumbled as bombs fell nearby, blasting out all of the windows and smashing in the roof. We had to move out of this house too, as it was now unlivable.

I really do not like to remember those times at all, but in the following pages I will share my story in detail with you.

Figure 2. Adolf Hitler performing the Nazi salute.

Maria Rosa

The "Jewish Letters"

I was six years old when I started my first year of elementary school, in 1938-39. As our town was a holiday resort, there were no community schools nearby; it had plenty of hotels and restaurants, as well as fancy houses, but it didn't have any schools. So every morning, I donned my heavy backpack and walked uphill for approximately two hours to get to the next town, which was located at a higher elevation. This trek was repeated daily - winter, summer, rain or snow.

In our first year of school, we learned the alphabet and how to write. The cursive writing they taught us at this time was called *Kurrentschrift,* or Kurrent writing, otherwise known as *Altedeutscheschrift* (Old German Script), which was based on late medieval cursive or blackletter gothic writing. It had been used for hundreds of years, persisting even until the mid 20th century, even though many of the individual letters acquired variant forms over time.

Learning to read and write properly in Kurrent was considered mandatory for students in the first year of school, in order to graduate to second grade – which was deemed an absolute must, so most children accomplished it.

As I entered second grade in 1939/40, our entire school system was in the process of being changed. After the Nazis seized power in Austria, the Kurrent writing was banned by decree of the German Reich's Minister of Arts and Education. They called this old form of writing the "Schwabacher Jewish Letters."

On January 3, 1941 the Nazis declared a public regulation, the *Normalschrifterlass*, in which book

To Hell and Back

printing in *Kurrentschrift* was banned and an official replacement decreed. A letter in this regard was circulated by the government:

"On behalf of the Führer I notify for common attention that:

"Regarding and calling the so-called gothic typeface as a German typeface is wrong. In fact, the gothic typeface consists of Jew-letters from Schwabach. Like they later gained control of the newspapers, the Jews

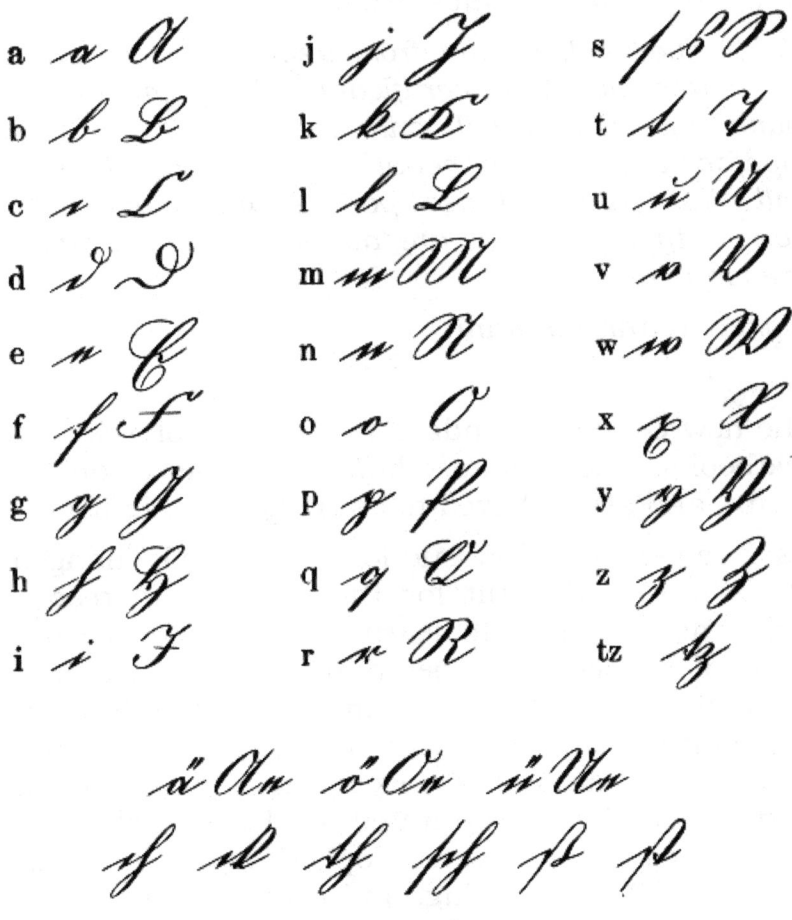

Figure 3. Kurrentschrift, or Kurrent writing.

living in Germany had seized control over the printing shops at introduction of the printing press, so that the Schwabacher Jew-letters were heavily introduced in Germany.

"Today the Führer decided in a meeting with Reichsleiter Max Amann and book printing shop owner Adolf Müller, that the Antiqua typeface is to be called the normal typeface in future. Step by step all printing products have to be changed to this normal typeface. As soon as this is possible for school books, in schools only the normal typeface will be taught.

"Authorities will refrain from using the Schwabacher Jew-letters in future; certificates of appointment, road signs and similar will only be produced in normal typeface in future. On behalf of the Führer, Mr. Amann will first change those papers and magazines to normal typeface, that are already spread abroad or are wanted to be.

Signed Martin Bormann"

The new German standard for our school writing and textbooks, the *Normalschrift*, was based on Latin script, and also referred to as *Ausgangsschrift*.

As I remember, this sudden and rapid changeover made it very difficult for the children to read and write, as they had to learn a whole new form and style of cursive alphabet and typeface. We had to start all over again, repeating the entire first grade curriculum with our new Nazi-approved script. Of course, the parents were extremely upset about this, and the children continued to have problems for years to come. However, I applied myself diligently to learning the new writing, and soon caught up in the second grade.

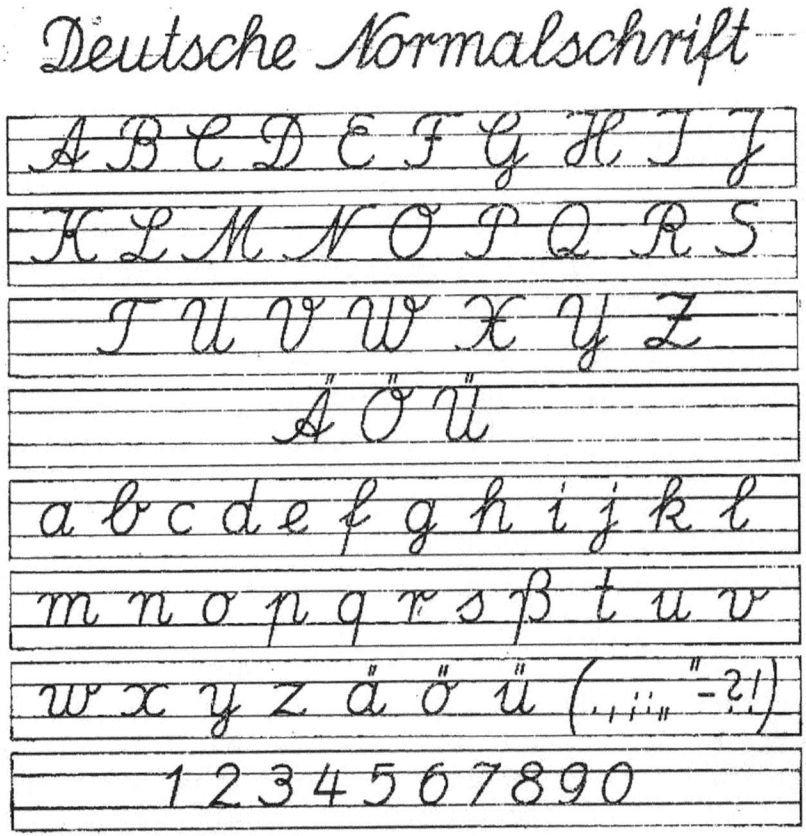

Figure 4. Normalschrift, or German standard writing.

Maria Rosa

Love Between Jews and Gentiles

Now I will tell the tragic love story of a Jewish man and a Gentile woman. The lady, born in 1903, happened to be my father's sister, and my grandmother's first daughter. Her name was Therese, but we usually called her "Risa."

When Aunt Risa was 24 years old, she met a young Jewish gentleman in our town, and he was quite taken in with her. He was a businessman, and as Risa also came from a quite well-to-do business family, it wasn't long before they got married and started their new home together.

He was involved in the lumber industry, and business evidently was good. They built a large, beautiful villa on a nearby hill, and furnished it together. I still remember the gorgeous and elegant furnishings - the white French Provincial bedroom set, the pretty chandeliers, the luxurious carpet; they were reminiscent of one of the rooms in the imperial palace in Vienna. I visited many times, and to me it was just like being in Fairyland!

In 1928 a son was born to them, named Fred. He spent a lot of time at Grandmother's house, and so did my brother and I, so we pretty much grew up together. We played together, explored together, fought together, and hugged each other, without a second thought. We were quite a happy family. My relatives on Grandmother's side were devoted Catholics, but religion never played much of a role in the lives of her children. Love, understanding, and happiness always came first.

Fred was about 8-9 years old when Risa came home one day, crying sorrowfully on her mother's shoulder.

She said that her husband has to leave. This was around 1937-38.

I remember Risa emptying out her house in a panic, and hauling as much of the furniture as she could over to Grandmother's place. After her husband left, the house was taken over by perfect strangers. We didn't know who they were – obviously outsiders, not people from town.

Even though the local townspeople were aware little Fred was half-Jewish, nobody cared! Most Gentile families in town were friends with Jewish families. But when the Nazis took over Austria in 1939, things changed a great deal. We personally knew at least three nice Jewish families, who were friends we sadly lost and never heard from again.

Before the war started, our Jewish friends owned large villas with extensive gardens, and we always enjoyed their company and hospitality. Those families were by the name of Andauer, Ashkenazi, and Nürnberger. I was still only a young child during the war, but after a while I began to ask my mother, "How come we don't visit there anymore?" And I was told, "Oh, they had to leave. They had to go away." Their homes, too, were soon taken over by outsiders.

My grandmother's husband had already died in 1936, so during the war she had very little help; she was mostly on her own as far as caring for her family was concerned. After Fred's father had to leave, she arranged a special room for her grandson, with a customized student desk. As far as I can understand, Fred was home-schooled and hidden away from authorities as much as possible. He was allowed to go outside to play with us once in a while, to explore the woods, pick berries, and stroll along the rivers and such; but as far as everything else was concerned, this boy – a cute little kid with wavy hair – was always kept discretely in the background.

I still see him in my mind's eye today, sitting at his little desk with his small plate of food. He was such a polite little boy, that every time he got something to eat he said, "Thank you very much, Omi (Grandma)."

Unfortunately, Fred never heard from his father again. He grew up as a child with only one parent, with Grandmother doing her best to substitute for the second. After losing her home, Aunt Risa also moved back into her mother's house with Fred. She cried a lot and was very unhappy, waiting day after day for news and correspondence from her husband that never arrived. His situation apparently remained a mystery.

Risa died fairly young, probably out of grief, so Fred ultimately ended up living alone with Grandmother. My father, who was Fred's uncle, also helped out quite a bit financially.

The last time I saw Fred, when I was about 14 years old, he was a young man by then. Grandmother told me that he had joined the police force. Determined to find his father, Fred searched for many years, but to no avail.

Figure 5. A Nazi march.

Close Calls with My Brother

I have no sisters, and only one brother. He was born in 1936, making him four years my junior. I still remember the day Mom went to the hospital with labor pains when I was 4 years old. My brother arrived a month early due to complications; in fact, the doctor told my father that he couldn't save both of them. But after Father's urgent plea, the physician managed to accomplish this monumental feat.

As a result, my brother was very little and puny-looking until he was about 7. His first school year was delayed due to his small stature and poor health. My mom definitely had her hands full with him, as he was unruly as well.

My brother and I used to run freely through the meadows, woods, and rivers near the beautiful summer resort town. It was idyllic there, just like you would see in a picture book. Little Frankie, always very adventurous and playful, got himself into a lot of trouble. He never considered the possibility of danger lurking around the corner. He took many daring risks and evidently did not understand the potential consequences.

My mother expected me, a little girl, to look after Frank at all times. Despite my best efforts, he dragged me into a number of scary situations. The first happened when he was about 5 years old: we were living in a house with an orchard in the back, enclosed by a big fence with a hinged gate that was left half-open.

As soon as little Frank found my mother's bicycle in the yard, he immediately grabbed it and attempted to ride. He ran toward the gate, stepped on the pedal and swung himself over the seat. He awkwardly tried to pedal through the gate, but failed and fell sideways instead. I screamed with horror as the metal hinge of the gate went right through his chin – in through the bottom and out on top. OUCH!!!

This was no doubt a very dangerous situation, but luckily there were some skilled doctors and surgeons in town who were able to sew him up. Frank eventually recovered, albeit with a large scar under his chin.

Now for the second episode – again, I always had to watch out for my little brother, and if something happened to him it was inevitably "my fault."

I went swimming quite frequently, not far from home, in a slow-flowing canal about ten feet deep. The water was clear and inviting, but of course, it was no wading pool; only proficient swimmers would dare to jump in. So one day Frank and I were playing ball near the canal, then sitting together on a blanket with a board game. Suddenly, he grew distracted; then he stood up with a mischievous smile, ran toward the canal, and jumped right in.... but he couldn't swim!

Now, I was still just a little girl myself, 10 or 11 years old. I screamed for help, but nobody was around, so I jumped into the canal after him. With much effort, I was able to fish him out before he drowned. Thank heavens! My mother would have never forgiven me.

I remember the third close call with crystal clarity, even to this very day. It still gives me cold shivers just to think about it: My brother and I used to go strawberry-picking at the base of a big rocky hill. Luckily we didn't encounter any snakes, although there were a lot of fire ants crawling around, ready to painfully sting at the slightest disturbance. Otherwise, it was quite a lovely place to go hunting for those sweet, juicy wild strawberries.

Sometimes, we would hear voices and strange noises coming from the other side of the hill. One day our curiosity got the better of us, and we decided to climb up the slope to investigate. It was huge really, perhaps one block wide, and quite steep as well.

As we reached the top and glanced over the edge, we discovered a stone quarry on the other side. The craggy scarp below went down at least a hundred feet, if not more. Here, workers were digging and excavating for marble and other expensive raw materials.

Losing interest, we trudged back down the hill to pick strawberries as usual. I followed closely behind my brother, always keeping a watchful eye on him. After awhile, I simply glanced down at my fruit basket for a moment, checking what I had harvested so far. When I looked up, all of a sudden I couldn't see him...

I screamed, "FRAAANKK!!!!" He hollered back, but oh God – I could not figure out where he was! His cries echoed back and forth against the rocks, yet seemed to emanate from very close by. I followed his yells as best I could, finding myself headed toward the top of the hill above the quarry. And there he was, hanging on a rock about two feet away from the edge!

I urgently pulled him back, saving his life for the second time. It was probably just a matter of seconds before both of us would have fallen to our deaths, down a hundred-foot-deep quarry pit. I earnestly hoped he wouldn't tell our mother!

Of course, whenever she found out that Frank had done something wrong, I was the one who received the blame, along with a lot of painful spankings from her. I was supposed to be the "big girl," the guardian who was responsible for whatever he did wrong – which I really didn't think was fair. I was just a little child too – how could I protect him?

Life wasn't all fun and games however. As the war intensified, both of us children suffered a lot, and not only because of food and other shortages. We could hear the air raid sirens blaring daily throughout our town. Every single day, over and over again, the sirens warned us of approaching warplanes. We were constantly on edge, and it got to the point where every little noise started to scare us.

The moment the sirens began blasting, we would pack whatever food we had, along with blankets or other supplies, and dart into a tunnel running underneath a railroad track. This tunnel had a little brook flowing through it, so at least there was fresh water, but sometimes it was completely dark. Then we would sit and hide in that gloomy tunnel, sometimes for five to six hours at a time, because we were afraid to go home.

I remember one particular townswoman, a mother of three babies, who often joined us in the tunnel. She already packed up her supplies in the early morning hours, anticipating the same routine each day. She would only return home in the dark of night, after a day spent mostly in hiding with her children. I don't know how she ever did it.

What Frank and I experienced as children left us with a lot of post-traumatic stress. When I was in my teens, I began to scream every night in my sleep, loud enough to wake my father. I was having recurring nightmares about the war, and my brother suffered from the same problem. It was many years before these ceased entirely, but the memories still haunt us even today.

Holy Smoke

When I was in elementary school, we were required to learn about our Catholic religion and attend Mass every Sunday. There was no separation of church and state like there is in the USA, and Catholicism was the official religion. So on weekends, we visited a little stone chapel in the town of Eichberg. This chapel belonged to the mountainous Castle Aichberg, an imposing stronghold in the province of Styria.

The medieval castle was built in the late 12th century, after wars with Hungary in which the border was demarcated along the path of the river Lafnitz. The castle was first called Burg Aichberg in 1374, after one of its original owners, Konrad von Aichberg. In 1378, Wulfing von Aichberg built the nearby chapel of stone, which became the parish church.

The castle has a turbulent history, having endured many rapid changes of ownership, political and economic declines, and several renovations. During the First World War, the castle housed Galician refugees who dismantled the roof to obtain firewood. Near the end of World War II, Burg Aichberg was used for quartering the German army.

I clearly remember looking up at the tall stone foundations of the castle, and the wealth inside the little chapel – the golden chalices, saintly décor, and antique paintings. Whenever the priest would swing his oversized censer in this small building, the incense smoke grew so thick that one nearly suffocated and choked, and couldn't see beyond the hazy outline of one's neighbor in the next seat. The chapel had practically no air circulation, so I always hurried to escape this acrid cloud as soon as possible, never understanding why the thoughtless priest seemingly wanted to asphyxiate his parishioners.

In 1939, Hitler instituted a compulsory Church tax for Catholics in Austria, with a rate of 1.1%. This tax was retained after World War II, in order to keep the Church independent of political powers.

The last time I visited the chapel was in 1942, as I then had to transfer to a different school. Since 1986 the castle and chapel have been privately owned and renovated, and the main building now houses a museum and art gallery.

Figure 6. Castle Aichberg and its little stone chapel, before renovations.

The Sanctuary

On our way to secondary school every morning, my schoolmates and I on our bicycles would pass by a very mysterious and ominous landmark. This imposing edifice was Burg Thalberg, an abandoned medieval castle. Thalberg Castle is an excellent example of high Middle Age architecture in Styria, and is one of the best-preserved Romanesque buildings in all of Austria.

The original structure was built in the late 1100s as part of a series of border fortifications against Hungarian invaders. In the 1500s, Burg Thalberg became the central hub of eastern Styria's Protestant Reformation movement and exercised legal dominion over the District Court, only to be partially destroyed soon after by roving bands of Ottoman Turks.

The castle had long stood as a defensive fortress and refuge for the town of Friedberg. One of its arched portals functioned strategically as a fortified pass, being the only accessible entryway between two nearby communities. My schoolmates and I would ride through this spooky overgrown archway every day - it was so dark inside that we would have to turn our bicycle lights on in order to see our way through!

We children were curious enough to attempt to explore the rest of the gloomy, forbidding ruins, but it was far too dark, and part of the castle interior had already collapsed.

The Turkish invaders tried to take the castle by force but were eventually defeated, and in 1610 the Jesuits of Graz, a Catholic order, took possession of the building. When the Jesuit order was dissolved in 1773, Castle Thalberg fell into the hands of the state

Figure 7. The ruins of Burg Thalberg.

and was leased out, eventually to be auctioned to new owners who allowed the structure to decay.

Every time it rained, my brother and I would run through the woods to reach a small chapel near the castle, called *Kapelle Heiligenbrunn* (Holy Water Chapel). Built in 1711, it used to be a Catholic pilgrimage site and was most likely constructed by the Jesuits who owned Burg Thalberg at the time. This quaint little building was surrounded by thick woods and featured a late Gothic Madonna statue upon the altar. Holy water from a natural spring flowed into a marble basin, and here we would refresh ourselves after gathering a load of fresh mushrooms, blueberries, and truffles that had sprung forth from the rain.

This was our beloved sanctuary, a special place that we kept hidden from the other children, lest they disturb our peace and swipe our harvest. After the war we could no longer return, as the surrounding area was littered with land mines.

Figure 8. Kapelle Heiligenbrunn.

For the Birds

Before the war, my father's brother Herman became a member of the Austrian resistance forces - the Home Guard or *Heimwehr*. For headgear, these soldiers wore a distinctive cap or hat decorated with the tail feathers of the black grouse, which were popularly hunted as game birds in the region of Tyrol. Because of this, they were nicknamed the "*Hahnenschwanzler*" ("Rooster Tails") and were ridiculed by their opponents with a satirical rhyme:

"Hahnenschwanzler, Hahnenschwanzler, you're a poor wretch,

What the cock has on his butt, you wear proudly on your head."

The *Heimwehr* was originally formed with the intention of defending the borders of Austria. They eventually came into strong opposition with the Nazi party because they believed Austria should remain an independent state, rather than being assimilated into the German *Reich*. Some violence ensued, and one particularly memorable incident included the Nazis throwing eggs at the *Heimwehr* during a march!

The Nazis eventually suppressed the Home Guard, and when the war began, Herman was drafted into the German army. After he got shipped off, all contact ceased and he seemingly disappeared, as no one ever heard from him again. Herman was my grandmother's second son, and she was truly heartbroken. All through the war she attempted to get more information about Herman, but to no avail.

At the end of the war, my grandmother's third son, Otto, was taken by the Soviets as a war prisoner and languished in a Russian prison until 1947 or '48. When he finally was allowed to return, his body was so bloated with water that he appeared twice his usual weight. He had received no medical attention and had been eating whatever scraps of rubbish he was able to scrounge up. Otto was very traumatized and didn't want to tell us much about what he had endured.

Figure 9. The Hahnenschwanzler.

Figure 10. The *Stephansdom* Cathedral in Vienna.

Yellow Armbands in Vienna

My mother was originally from Vienna, Austria. She was born and raised in this city of millions. Her own mother died when she was very young, so she was raised by her mother's sister, my great-aunt Anna. I spent a lot of time in Vienna with Aunt Anna between 1939-1942, when I was 7 to 10 years old.

I still remember Anna and her huge apartment in the Second District, called Leopoldstadt - the island between the Danube and the Danube Canal. This district was noted for its high percentage of Jewish inhabitants. Anna also had several children of her own. Often, Aunt Anna would take us all to visit or attend Mass at the magnificent St. Stephen's Cathedral, or *Stephansdom*, as she lived close by. This cathedral was (and still is) considered to be the Roman Catholic "mother church" of Vienna, and the seat of the Archbishop, so it practically felt like going on a special pilgrimage each time.

With its unique, multi-colored tile roof, this cathedral has borne witness to many important events in Austria's history. The *Stephansdom* is the oldest church in Vienna and is believed to have been built atop an ancient Roman cemetery and earlier sacred landmarks. Founded in 1137, the partially constructed Romanesque church was solemnly dedicated to Saint Stephen in 1147, shortly before embarking on the Second Crusade. Since then, the cathedral has been rebuilt, remodeled, and expanded several times.

Its massive south tower, affectionately nicknamed "Steffl" (little Stephen), is the highest and foremost feature of the Viennese skyline. Its construction was a 65 year undertaking, from 1368-1433. During the

1529 Siege of Vienna and the 1683 Battle of Vienna against the encroaching Ottoman Empire, the Steffl served as the main defensive observation and command post for what was then the walled city of Vienna. Even until 1955, the tower was manned by night watchmen, who rang bells if a fire was spotted. The imperial double-eagle emblem of the Hapsburg Empire, formerly ruled from Vienna, decorates both the south tower and the tiled roof.

The *Stephansdom* contains 18 gorgeous altars as well as many smaller chapels dedicated to various saints. Extensive catacombs run underneath the cathedral, and next to the entryway of the catacombs is a pulpit from which St. John Capistrano and Hungarian general John Hunyadi preached a crusade in 1456 to hold back Muslim invasions of Europe.

The sanctuary also features the Byzantine-style Maria Pötsch Icon from Hungary. This highly revered depiction of the Madonna and Child grew famous after two miraculous incidents in which the icon shed real tears, and hence came to be known as the "Weeping Madonna." It was brought to the cathedral under the orders of Emperor Leopold I, to keep it safe from Muslim armies that still controlled much of Hungary in 1696. The largest of the cathedral bells, the biggest in Austria, was originally cast in 1711 using metal from cannons captured from the Muslim invaders.

Wolfgang Amadeus Mozart had a close relationship with St. Stephen's, and was appointed music director shortly before his death. His funeral was held in the Chapel of the Cross inside.

During World War II, the commandant of the retreating German forces ordered Captain Gerhard Klinkicht to "fire a hundred shells and leave it in just debris and ashes." But the cathedral was narrowly saved from destruction when Captain Klinkicht disregarded these orders. Sadly however, as Russian troops entered Vienna in 1945, civilian looters started fires in nearby shops, which damaged the cathedral's roof and caused it to collapse. Protective brick shells had been built around the most valuable artworks, so many of these treasures were saved, but the beautifully-carved 15th century choir stalls and tile roof had to be rebuilt, and many of the towers and bells were also damaged.

I have very fond memories of visiting St. Stephen's with my aunt and her family, before it was marred by the fire. I also met Anna's husband Karl several times when I was smaller, but later on I was not able to see him anymore. Eventually, I worked up the courage to ask Anna where Karl was. She said he "had to leave," but wouldn't elaborate. At this time I realized that my other aunt Elizabeth's husband was gone, too.

I felt quite at home in Vienna, and my little brother and I spent a lot of time near the Danube, Austria's biggest river, playing in the grass on the banks. I don't quite remember when I first noticed Jewish women nervously walking around, wearing yellow armbands with a Star of David. They looked very glum, glancing downward in a dejected and beaten manner.

This was a surprise to me, so I asked Aunt Anna what the meaning of all this was, and why they wore those yellow armbands. My aunt told me they were Jewish people, and that was why her husband and her sister Elizabeth's husband had to leave.

I asked Anna, "Are they coming back soon?" and got only a sad smile.

Maria Rosa

The Nazi Takeover

At the beginning of the war, as time went by, more and more strangers came into town. There was one particularly hated man who was practically running the whole community. He looked like a giant to me, and his behavior resembled that of a nasty old ogre! He was the *Ortsgruppenleiter* or "Local Group Leader," a rank held by the head Nazi of a town or city. While traditional government titles such as *Burgermeister* or Town Mayor continued to exist, local town and city administration were usually overshadowed, if not entirely replaced, by the Nazi political system and corresponding leadership ranks, becoming little more than a rubber stamp to Nazi designs.

The position of *Ortsgruppenleiter* encompassed a large amount of responsibility and power during World War II, as it was these Nazi officials who typically ran the city civil defense systems as well as the allocation of war rations and civil relief efforts.

A lot of German women with their children also came into town, and the *Ortsgruppenleiter* assigned them to local housing. Most of these women, we learned, were Nazi officers' wives; they were widely disliked, as they were often very condescending and arrogant towards the native population.

Next door to us lived an Austrian man who was enlisted as a Nazi soldier during the war. After his wife died in childbirth, he married a German woman and moved her into his home. Despite his frequent absences while on duty, they had a child together, and when the little girl was about 2 years old I used to say to her, "Good morning, sweetie." Her constant reply of "*Leck Arsch! Leck Arsch!*" however, was far from sweet!

We grew quite scared and intimidated by this influx of strange people. At the same time, many of our old friends left and didn't come back. These were years of great uncertainty and confusion for countless families. After the war, many of the people who had been overseeing the town disappeared, which was to be expected.

Backing up for a moment, I would like to talk more about the town where I lived during the war. You may have been wondering why a small community – which was actually a holiday resort with restaurants, villas, and so forth – got bombed.

We citizens were also flabbergasted and couldn't understand why. It remained an infuriating mystery throughout the duration of the war. But later on, the puzzle was solved: Every day, we saw open wagons being dragged through town, carrying pails full of old cloths, rags, and other seemingly innocent old junk. They were taken to a certain spot, and nobody thought twice about it. We were told that these materials were for clothing manufacture, and the clothes were designated for distribution to the soldiers and civilian population.

After the war, we found out that this "clothing manufacturing facility" was actually a Nazi-run munitions factory. This was the only reason we got bombed, and the population who suffered as a result was never even aware of, nor approved of, such operations in the first place.

Maria Rosa

Mortar Strudel

After the undercover munitions factory was discovered by the Allied forces, our town was bombed severely. Many homes were irreparably damaged by the sheer destructive force of the pressure and shock waves emanating from the nearby detonations. The explosions were also extremely loud, so many innocent people's hearing was damaged by these blasts.

One day my grandmother, a gourmet chef, baked a beautiful *Krautstrudel* (cabbage strudel) for our family. She laid it on the dinner table shortly before we were about to sit down for lunch. We were all very much looking forward to eating and spending time together. All of a sudden –

-- BAM!! The entire house shook with a deafening rumble and glass shards flew at us from the broken windows. Shingles dropped down from the roof, and half a foot of mortar rained down from the ceiling, piling up on top of the strudel.

A bomb had been dropped down the street, a mere few hundred feet away from our home. Not only was our lunch completely ruined, but had the house not been built from stone, it would have surely collapsed on us. We were deeply disturbed by this event, and quickly ran downstairs to take cover. A further series of blasts shook the house. Afterward, I saw my mother crawling out from underneath the dust and debris, covered in mortar, looking white as a ghost.

In the meantime, my father was gone most of the time. Since he had a heart condition, he was never a combat soldier. Instead, he was assigned to do car and motor maintenance for some officers. We saw him only once or twice a year during the war, for a short period of time.

I will never forget the day when my father returned carrying one banana for me. I had never seen a banana in my life up till this point, much less a chocolate bar; so to me, this single piece of sweet, exotic fruit was like a gift from heaven!

Nazi Encounters

Ever since my childhood in Austria, many annoying and disconcerting episodes from the Nazi occupation and Second World War have stuck in my mind. Several things happened that I could never understand - but today I do.

When I was in secondary school, items such as shoes, socks, house slippers, etc. were very scarce. So one of our "special" school assignments was to sew slippers made out of cornhusks. We started the project in our handicraft classes, and then we had to finish at home.

In order to weave those slippers, we had to braid the cornhusks over a wooden shoe-form, and then lined them with warm insulating materials. The technique required the use of a needle, and of course I did not have a thimble, so I ended up with bloody fingers every time I worked on this.

Now, I needed house slippers myself, but I wasn't allowed to keep them. We had to hand our homemade masterpieces over to a person who was collecting them "for the soldiers." But I doubt very much that any soldier was running around in house slippers made of cornhusks: later on we found out that these slippers were given to the German women and their children.

The second incident, which infuriated my mother and grandmother, occurred in the small holiday resort town where I was raised. On certain Sundays, our community was visited by an ear-splittingly loud hillbilly oompah band. This band was made up of six to eight homespun wannabe-Nazis, all banging away deafeningly on their cymbals, bass drums, tubas, and trombones for the support and "honor" of the German

Figure 11. Woven cornhusk slippers.

Reich. They paused in front of every house expecting charitable donations, and if they received none they would continue playing as rambunctiously as they could, busting the eardrums of every resident until they received a contribution.

On other Sundays, the new so-called town "leaders," whoever they were – certainly not natives – went around to some homes and demanded entry, examining every stovetop to see what was cooking. Only one pot was allowed per household. The Nazis called this day *Eintopfsonntag*, which means One Pot Sunday. On one Sunday per month, citizens were expected to eat a one-pot meal and contribute their savings to charities benefitting the *Reich*. A German propaganda photo showed Adolf Hitler and Joseph Goebbels sharing a meal on "One Pot Sunday," with the pot in the foreground:

If you were cooking more than one pot, the noticeably over-fed inspectors wanted to know from where you got the food. Our family never had anything confiscated, as we didn't have much food anyhow. But we did hear from other families, farmers and so forth, that a lot of such interrogation was going on, although I don't know what happened if a second pot was discovered. I thought it was absolutely

Figure 12. Nazi propaganda photo of Adolf Hitler and Joseph Goebbels sharing a meal on "One Pot Sunday."

ridiculous, and my mother and grandmother were just infuriated by it all; so much so that every time the Nazi inspectors left, they pointed the "long nose" after them – the Austrian equivalent of the middle finger.

My family deeply disliked what was happening. Soon, we discovered that the oompah musicians who had collected the money would visit the pub in the evening, sitting for hours at their *Stammtisch* – an informal gathering where they would socialize, play cards, discuss topics of interest, and guzzle beer from large *steins*. It was anyone's guess as to how much money actually went to charity.

Towards the end of the war, when I was 12 years old, my mother suddenly got very ill. I learned later on that the women of the community were ordered by the Nazis to dig ditches surrounding the town as "troops were approaching the borders." No one would inform us as to which troops, or what was happening, and we were forbidden to listen to any news on the radio, except for Nazi propaganda. It was strictly prohibited, with punishment of fine or imprisonment. As they dug these ditches, the women were standing in water up to their hips, and many became sick as a result. My mother ended up with severe pneumonia and all kinds of other health problems. She was never the same after that.

I could describe many other such instances, but you can pretty much infer from this how native Austrians were treated by the Nazi German occupiers. There were numerous Germans in our town, supervising the population, but we never knew who those people were or what they were planning, so our family kept fairly quiet and tried not to provoke anyone. My mother was more bold and forward though, so when she had something to say she said it, even at her own risk, as she found this way of life very frustrating. After the war was over, I heard my mother and grandmother say many times that they were so happy things were going to change.

Figure 13. German oompah band.

Maria Rosa

Identified Flying Objects

As the fighting intensified, Nazi fighter planes and Allied bombers skirmished in the skies. During one particularly violent battle over a nearby town near the end of 1944, an Allied bomber was ambushed by Nazi forces. In order to gain speed to escape, the bomber suddenly dropped its cargo.

This cargo unfortunately consisted of a number of active bombs which exploded upon impact with the ground, accidentally killing several innocent children and adults as a result. To our grief, our secondary school required us students to attend their funeral. It was such a morose and depressing affair that I have never been able to visit a cemetery since that time - I am always reminded of the war and the helpless children who became "unavoidable collateral damage."

By 1945, we were praying daily for the war to finish. Russian troops were approaching the nearby border with Hungary, and Hungarian refugees were streaming in from the east. In March, my father convinced his superior to help us leave for our own safety. Soon we took refuge to the south in the city of Graz, staying overnight with numerous other families while waiting for transportation to take us west to get closer to the Allied troops.

We got very little sleep, as military operations were in full swing for most of the night. The sky above Graz was lit up like a Christmas tree by burning flares which had been dropped to illuminate more bombing targets below. In the morning, we were lucky enough to find the same young mother with her three children who had been hiding in the railway tunnel with us during air raids. She now drove an old flatbed truck, and agreed to take us with her to the west.

We were forced to drive only by night, because fighter planes were shooting at people and moving vehicles during the day. Even with this precaution, three low-flying Spitfires spotted us, mistaking us for an enemy military vehicle, and decided to attack us as we sat unarmed and helpless in the back of a gray, medium-sized truck.

As the planes swooped down, they began to shoot at us - a moving target full of women and children. We screamed in terror and ducked as ammunition flew past. At the very last moment, we drove into a dark tunnel and escaped.

It was just a matter of seconds before we would have been mincemeat, so we really had our guardian angels with us that night. My little brother, who was four years younger than me, to this very day is telling me how he can never forget that. He was utterly terrified, and considered us extremely fortunate to survive.

Figure 14. Supermarine Spitfires flown during World War II.

Maria Rosa

Refugees of War

We managed to escape to a small town in another province of Austria. Fortunately, we found a room we could stay in so that we had a roof over our heads. Announcements in town heralded the approach and imminent arrival of the Allied troops. We prayed and anxiously awaited the day they would come.

In the meantime, my mother did everything possible for us to survive. In spite of the nearby farming community there was very little food available, and we had nothing to barter in exchange. The imminent end of the war was a real blessing to us, but it was also a time when we lost everything, including our home. We had no money, very little food, and nothing else but the clothes on our backs. As refugees, we were mostly dependent on the kindness and generosity of perfect strangers. We were only allowed to stay in our borrowed room because my father knew the homeowner and had previously made arrangements with him before we fled.

We were not able to communicate with my grandmother at this time, as she had remained back in the previous town, which was occupied by Soviet troops. She was busy taking care of Fred, and many were scared as news of Soviet war crimes spread. Unfortunately, my father was also not with us. We had no idea where he was, or if he was even alive at this point. All we could do was wait.

In the woods nearby, I found a gigantic heap of German money (*Reichsmark*) on the ground. One might think that this was like winning the lottery, but far from it: this money was now so worthless, due to devaluation, that the whole pile couldn't even buy a slice of bread. So the people had just thrown it away, like so much trash. Shopping in stores was a thing of the past.

Near the end of April, we finally got some help from the town mayor, who directed us on how to obtain ration books. With these, we were told, we could get rice, sardines, and white bread from international aid operations that will arrive in our area after the Allied forces move in.

I still remember the horrible, disgusting bread we ate during the war – it was bitter to the taste, and would fall apart when you tried to slice it. Later on, we found out that the dough had been mixed with sawdust, ground chestnuts, acorns, and anything else that could be used as "filler," because wheat flour was so scarce. Anyone who consumed this awful dross was lucky not to get sick and throw up!

The mayor informed us that we could only obtain our ration books in the county capital, a much larger and distant city. My little brother was approximately 9 years old, and Mom could not leave him all alone, as he was still getting himself into trouble all the time. So she befriended another female refugee who was also a mother, and sent the two of us off to the capital many miles away, to collect our ration books.

Maria Rosa

Abandoned in the Alps

At this time, there was no motorized transportation available to us – no bus, no car, nothing at all. Instead, we had to use pedal power. My companion and I each borrowed a bicycle, and we started pedaling in the early morning hours toward the county capital. Fortunately, I was already a good cyclist – I was used to riding to school, even on icy roads in the middle of winter.

But this trip was far more challenging: we would have to pedal about 70 - 80 miles up and down twisting Alpine roads.

All I had with me was one apple, a dry piece of bread, and some devaluated money that was still absolutely worthless. We pedaled like crazy all day long, knowing it would be about seven hours before we'd arrive at our faraway destination.

The woman who rode beside me was older, probably in her late 30s or early 40s. She complained about getting tired, but so was I. We were both hungry. So of course, during our journey I ate my apple and my dry piece of bread, which was my only meal for the day.

Finally we reached the city, winded and weary, and just before closing time we received our ration books. We had no choice but to stay overnight, since a return trip the same day would have been impossible. We were exhausted, hungry, and a frosty coldness was encroaching on the air. The weather at this high altitude had not yet warmed up, as it was still only the end of April.

I don't remember where I fell asleep, but I awoke in the morning with a shock: I was all by myself. I searched for hours for my lady companion, but I could not find her anywhere. Apparently, she had abandoned me.

Now, I still had nothing whatsoever to eat. I attempted to buy something, anything, from any place that was open – a restaurant, a market, a café, it didn't matter. I begged them all to accept my cash in exchange for anything available. But I couldn't even buy a cold potato or a piece of bread with my money. It was hopeless.

At this point, I was so desperately hungry that I was looking on the sidewalk for dandelions or grass or anything I could eat. Eventually, I decided that the only thing I could do was grab my bicycle and pedal another 70 miles back home by myself. This would surely take another 7 to 8 miserable hours, accented by my empty growling stomach.

Figure 15. Cold alpine road.

Pedaling for Life

As I continued to pedal, I grew very weak. I was still constantly looking to the side of the road for any type of edible flower or leaf I could chew, but with no luck. I rode for 3 – 4 hours in the Alpine cold, becoming ever more hungry and exhausted.

All of a sudden, a man on a bicycle appeared behind me, seemingly out of nowhere.

We were on a long country road, forlorn and isolated, with nobody to turn to for help. Looking over my shoulder, I saw that this man continued to follow me, gradually edging closer. I was scared out of my wits – where did he come from, I asked myself, and *what the heck does he want???*

With all my remaining adrenaline-fueled strength, I pedaled faster and faster until my legs felt like they were going to fall off. With great relief, I observed that my pursuer was not able to catch up with me, as he was an older guy, perhaps in his late 40s. Perhaps he didn't have any bad intentions, but as a 13-year-old girl all by myself, I was very glad to escape this encounter.

By the time I arrived home at 7 o'clock in the evening, it was already dark and my body felt like it was falling apart. I was starving of course, so my mom brought me some warm milk. My stomach was so sensitive that I promptly threw it up. It took me several days to get back to normal.

Victory Day

I still remember clearly the events on May 8th, 1945, when I was 13 years old. This was Victory Day in Europe, a day we had been anticipating with much joy. The Allies had formally accepted Nazi Germany's unconditional surrender, thus marking the end of Hitler's Third Reich, as well as the end of World War II in Europe. Hitler had already committed suicide on April 30 during the Battle of Berlin, so the surrender of Germany was authorized by his successor. People were cheering throughout the world, and British Prime Minister Winston Churchill waved to crowds gathered in London after broadcasts throughout the United Kingdom that the war with Nazi Germany was over. This was certainly one of the happiest days of my life.

The rations, although meager, were a real blessing for us – and I had never seen such white bread before! After all the starving we had done, this soft white bread covered with a small slice of creamy butter and a meaty sardine on top was like heaven!

The house we stayed in during the following months was situated right next to a walking path leading into the hills. The Allied soldiers had a base camp in the town below, and in their spare time they would walk up this path and explore the surrounding areas, passing by our home. We soon become friends with them. With my four years of school English, I was able to understand and communicate a little bit; some of the soldiers found this entertaining or even a bit nostalgic, as they had been away from their homes and families for an extended period of time.

Figure 16. Prime Minister Winston Churchill waves to London crowds on Victory Day.

I still fondly remember Tom from Australia. He made himself at home right away - even to the extent of chopping wood, cooking, and doing other things to help us. He told me he had served time as a prisoner in Australia, so he was simply cherishing his freedom and the ability to socialize with other friendly people.

Despite his checkered past, he was one of the nicest guys I had ever met. And one day, he brought me a huge surprise: the first piece of chocolate I had seen in four years! I was delighted, and oh how much I enjoyed it! Now I thought Tom was simply wonderful.

Of course, I also heard the Allied soldiers using many English words I hadn't heard before. Curious as I was, after eavesdropping on a little tirade littered with curse words starting with the letter f, I asked

Tom what this all meant. He smirked at me, but refused to explain. I think I embarrassed him. Oops!

My family and I spent about six months in this Alpine town, not yet able to return to our Soviet-occupied hometown. News was grim – we heard many stories of fighting, property and infrastructure damage, land mines, sickness, crime, and overall misery. Finally, my father resurfaced around the beginning of October.

He had walked week after week through the woods, from one province to the next, to get back to us. Carrying his mechanic's tool case, he had survived by working his way through, doing electrical and mechanical repairs for any person he met in exchange for food and brief shelter. The German *Reichsmarks* he took with him were still completely worthless; he had been unable to buy anything, including food, so he had lost a lot of weight as well. The mountains of discarded cash abandoned in the woods were only good for making bonfires. Despite these hardships, it was a joyful reunion.

Maria Rosa

The Stainless Steel Pot

During this chaotic time, Austria not only had no currency, but also no real government or law enforcement. In some ways, one could say it resembled the Wild West. Austria was eventually divided into four sectors, each occupied by a different nation. By the time we returned home at the end of September 1945, the Russians had pulled back, making way for the Allied troops.

At first, we were overjoyed at the prospect of coming back home. My grandmother was still living in her old house with my cousin. But of course, we soon discovered that everything else had changed. The Soviets had left behind a great deal of misery, poverty, and many fearful and traumatized civilians, especially women and children.

Our old home was now occupied by strangers, and all of our belongings were gone. When we fled, we were only able to take one suitcase with us. Everything else had disappeared, and even our house no longer belonged to us. My mother was inconsolable – how could we survive?? Grandmother, in her great kindness, made space for us to move into her home.

While cooking over the hot stove, Mother reminisced about her most priceless possession, now lost: a large set of stainless steel cookware, given to her by her father-in-law as a wedding present back in 1931. To appease her, Father searched all over town to find out who had stolen our belongings, in the hopes of recovering this expensive set of cookware.

After much effort, he only managed to find one lonely stainless steel pot, stored in a neighbor's house. He quickly reclaimed it and excitedly returned it to my mother.

It was just a regular pot – certainly not extraordinary; nothing that would have any real meaning for most people. But for my mother, this nostalgic utensil was the only extant reminder of her wedding, and of better times before a miserable war full of fear, hunger, and suffering.

When I visited my mother in Austria some years later, she told me to take the pot with me, as a memento of my upbringing. I have had this vessel now for 50 years. Whenever life seems to grow too challenging, I contemplate this pot as a reminder of how lucky we really are to be living in the United States.

I remind myself that there is always hope. There is always another tomorrow; a brand new day, with all of its opportunities and surprises.

So never give up!

Figure 17. The stainless steel pot.

Maria Rosa

The Kaiser's Bridge

After the return home, I needed to resume my enrollment in secondary school. The campus was again located a long distance away, so I was hoping to jump on the train on my way to school. But I was met with another grim surprise:

All regional rail services had been cancelled indefinitely, due to an infrastructure disaster - the Zeilbrücke had been destroyed!

The Zeilbrücke had been a key railway bridge carrying steam engines across the Lafnitz valley, connecting Graz with Vienna. It was built in 1903 by a corporation called *G. Ernst und Alb. Buss & Company*.

As can be seen in the old photo, the Zeilbrücke is a lenticular fishbelly truss bridge, spanning 235 meters in length. It is supported by three columnar pillars, each 32 meters high, built from stone masonry with cement foundations. The pillars measure about 7 meters in circumference at the base and taper off toward the top, where the three sections of ironwork are connected.

Before the bridge could be built, many negotiations with the government of the Austro-Hungarian Empire were necessary, beginning in 1901. On June 6, 1901 a regional railway construction project, of which the Zeilbrücke was part, met with the official approval of Emperor Franz Joseph I, the Kaiser himself. The bridge was soon recognized to be of great strategic and commercial value for the area.

On account of its tremendous size, elegant structure, and brilliant design, the Zeilbrücke was already considered an architectural wonder of its time, and

Figure 18. The Zeilbrücke before World War II.

an unmistakable testimony to the special talent and skill of the engineers working around the turn of the century.

From 1942 to spring of 1945, on my route to secondary school I would take the steam train whenever I could. But the bridge itself also attracted a lot of attention of a different sort: as mischievous kids will not miss an opportunity, I joined many other children running playfully over the Zeilbrücke when the trains were off-schedule. Such a game was obviously very dangerous and stupid, as there was only six feet of open space between the train track and the edge of the bridge. We were insane!

At the foot of the Zeilbrücke ran a pristine river with a small waterfall and a pond below. We went swimming there many times, and on the other side of the waterfall we watched with delight as the beavers built their dams. We would also go fishing and collect river rocks, peering curiously through the crystal clear water for anything of interest.

I still remember a day around the end of 1944, when the train was attacked by some low-flying fighter aircraft. Loads of hungry people from Vienna were using the trains on a daily basis, hoping to barter their goods and valuables for some fresh food in the surrounding farm communities. They hung like grapes from the sides of the overcrowded trains, quite likely terrified as they peered over the edge of the Zeilbrücke, holding on for dear life.

By 1945 we had left this area, escaping several weeks before the end of the war. German troops were already stationed in town. When the Russians neared, the Nazi army withdrew and blew up the middle section of the Zeilbrücke as part of their military strategy. Traffic was interrupted for many years, until the bridge could be rebuilt.

One can see that the modern reconstruction looks much the same as the original version. The old steam engine has been replaced by diesel trains and more modern technologies. A new road was built underneath, and the river was entirely diverted in order to serve a noisy, dusty sawmill – much to the annoyance of the original inhabitants of the area. Only empty fields of grass remain.

Figure 19. The Zeilbrücke in modern times.

Shifting Sands

I missed most of my third year of secondary school due to the war, so I had to make up for it in my last year. As if that wasn't difficult enough, our school was subjected yet again to major changes and reforms; all of the teachers that we had previously been acquainted with were gone. An entirely new set of faculty came in, as well as a different Principal and administration.

As I grew a little older I hoped we would all be able to return to some semblance of a peaceful existence again, like the one we had before the *Anschluss*. But the war had wrought irreparable changes.

Life in our hometown just wasn't the same anymore. Signs of wartime fighting were still evident everywhere; many apartments had been emptied out and stripped bare, leaving absolutely nothing inside. The walls of my grandmother's house were littered with large holes. Portions of other buildings had entirely collapsed. Our days were often filled with hunger, cold, and apprehension about what was going to happen next.

Our currency was still worthless, so all the stores had closed, as no business could be conducted. Bartering with the local farmers was the only way to obtain food. Shortages were so severe that people came from as far away as Vienna to trade expensive jewelry for a bag of potatoes. There was no soap, no paper, nor any household goods available. Students had to make do with whatever they could.

My brother and I wished we could go and pick berries and mushrooms in the woods again - but we were now forbidden to return, as two local children had stepped on landmines and were tragically killed. Even the little "Holy Water Chapel" was now sadly off-limits for us.

My best-loved place to visit during this time was my great-grandfather's farm. To me, it looked like the biggest estate in the entire region. There I could eat a warm meal during the holidays and enjoy the loving company of my more distant relatives. As I reminisced over a juicy slice of Christmas ham, many wistful memories danced in my mind.

Great Grandfather was born in 1850, and had died in 1942 at the ripe old age of 92. I was about 9 or 10 years old the last time I saw him. I still remember his long gray beard, his black sparkling eyes, and his deep robust voice. He was always very kind to us, and took a particular liking to my mother.

The area was surrounded by several castles which, during the war, had housed Allied prisoners captured by the Nazis in 1943 during the Italian Campaign. To my knowledge, these particular prisoners were treated relatively well, in accordance with the human rights requirements of the Geneva Convention. Officers and higher-ranking personnel were generally treated with special privileges, despite struggles with shortages of food. (However, a small number of other Allied personnel were sent to Nazi concentration camps for a variety of reasons, including being Jewish. Others may have been subjected to brutalities, forced labor, and squalid conditions.) During the day, these prisoners were transported to nearby farms to work, then shipped back to the castles at night. Even so, I never saw any guards, or any type of harsh supervision, since escape would have placed the soldiers in worse circumstances. Part of the food grown and harvested was then claimed and redistributed by the Nazi regime.

To Hell and Back

I thought about my friend John, a captured Allied soldier from Australia. He was a high-ranking army officer who was housed in the castle near my great grandfather's farm. During the day he would take off his spic-and-span uniform to work in the fields and meadows, and otherwise help my extended family; then he would proudly get dressed again at night, when he returned to the castle.

To me, John was a very friendly and attractive man. He would teach me some English and show me pictures of his family back in Australia. At dinner, he sat next to me at the table. We had a great deal of fun together, and I promised that I would visit him after the war was over.

As years passed by, I would think of John whenever I returned to visit the farm with my grandmother, wondering if he was able to return to Australia and if I'd ever see him again.

Figure 20. Opera house in Graz, before renovations.

Maria Rosa

School Fiascos

After my last year of secondary school, I was sent to boarding school in Graz in 1946. I attended business college at Die Staatliche Handels-Schule an der Akademy. I was determined to complete my education, and had my family's support in this endeavor.

So from 1946-1948 I stayed in Graz while attending business college. These years were also very difficult for me, as I had to be mostly self-reliant. The program was very expensive, and my father needed me to return home as soon as possible to help him in business, so I had to complete a four-year program in two years.

I liked the school and focused hard on my studies, earning good grades and passing my exams. But my wardrobe was severely lacking; I had practically no clothes or shoes to wear. Eventually, my father ordered two suits to be tailor-made for me, one gray and one blue. I loved these and was very proud to wear them. Nevertheless, it was almost impossible to find any attractive, fashionable shoes. I had to make do with a heavy pair of mountain boots – I called them my clod-hoppers! While very utilitarian, I felt they were extremely unattractive.

Between bouts of studying and pondering the ugliness of my wafflestompers, many school-related memories came rushing back.

When I started first grade, I had been really anxious to learn how to read and write, as my mother had already prepared me a little by teaching me the letters of the alphabet. It turned out that I was naturally left-handed. This was never an issue at home; but as soon as my teacher noticed that I was left-handed, she was infuriated. She expected me to learn to write with my right hand instead. Of course, this was very difficult for me, as I was already used to writing with my left hand.

My teacher went on the proverbial war-path: she kept a strict eye on me, and every time she caught me writing with my left hand, she took out a big heavy wooden ruler and hit me right over the fingers. OUCH! Once, twice, three times – SMACK! as often as she caught me. Needless to say, little me was in tears. And not only this: the first time she caught me, it was one smack. The second time, two smacks; the third, three smacks; and so forth. By the time one week was over, my fingers were blue and swollen, and I was unable to write at all. My eager willingness to learn how to write quickly faded as the agonizing pain took over.

As soon as my mother noticed my bruised fingers, she questioned me about what was going on. Did I hurt myself? What was all this?? So I told her that I got punished in school for writing with my left hand. My mother fumed and stormed into the Principal's office with me, complaining about this abuse and showing him my injuries. Gladly, that was the end of my first grade teacher: the school administration had received other complaints about her, so she was immediately discharged.

This rather backwards teacher apparently adhered to the old superstition that left-handedness was a mark of the Devil. Of course, I must say that the new teacher who took her place, an older man, was much worse. So after this, my parents decided to leave well enough alone. Complaining was useless, and the final decision on the matter was that I just had to learn how to write with my right hand.

I can only imagine how much trauma a red-headed student would have gone through, since being a "ginger" was also considered a mark of the Devil in old wives' tales!

In my third year of elementary school, we had a young female teacher for "handicrafts" class. She was experienced in business, so teaching handicrafts was a very boring occupation for her. But she needed a job, and when she applied, she had to demonstrate to the Nazi-run hiring office that she was capable of some "womanly" skills and activities, in order to make herself "useful." She was then assigned to our school.

Despite her brilliant personality, she turned out to be a very strange teacher by "normal" standards. She was interested in everything other than handicrafts - like teaching us how to whistle! I thought this was hilarious, and very odd, but I never forgot how to whistle after that. At the same time, she would tell us adventure stories about her school years in Vienna, and describe all the entertaining dramas she had seen at the Opera House, and so forth. She was really quite sophisticated, so I got the distinct impression that teaching handicraft was truly not the right occupation for her. But we liked her anyhow; she always made us smile.

Another funny episode happened in my last year of secondary school, in 1945-46. Along with our compulsory courses, we had the choice of an elective on the side. All of my major subjects had already been covered, so I was undecided as to how I should spend my free hour. I figured I loved music, so why not take music lessons? We were promised that a professor from another school would come in part-time and give us a music lesson on such and such days.

I daydreamed about learning guitar or piano. What fun that would be! But when I told my instructor, there was no one available to teach these. So instead, I was assigned to the cello.

Now me, a small and slender girl, with a great big cello... I thought, "What a joke!" How awkward and ridiculous! I hated the cello anyways, so I refused to learn it. The same professor was able to teach shorthand, so he convinced me to take that class with him instead. And I am glad he did, because shorthand turned out to be extremely useful for me, especially while taking lecture notes in business school. I still use it even today, even though it looks very antiquated and impractical in comparison to our modern computer technology.

Now in business college, at the age of 16, going on 17, I had this one particular professor who said he "admired my beautiful handwriting." So at the end of the school year, he asked me if I would help him to write out graduation certificates for the students. I was trying to please the professor, so I thought "Sure, why not? It would be impolite to say no." He asked me to come to his apartment, which was located in a huge building across from the Academy.

I arrived at his private office with the intention only of working; of course, I was very young, innocent, and stupid – I knew next to nothing about relationships, as I had never dated before. Most of my time was spent immersed in my studies or attending the opera as part of my cultural education, not with casual socializing.

I had barely sat down at the work desk when he started to bend over me in an odd manner, a bit too close for comfort. I tried to ignore the awkwardness and prompted him to direct me where to start, so that he would sit down and get settled. But instead of answering me, he bent down closer and tried to kiss me!

Now, this was more than enough for me! I was young, I was inexperienced, but I wasn't a fool. Enraged, I slapped him and told him off in no uncertain terms, and stormed out of his apartment instantly. Had I reacted in any other way, I knew what was coming. When I next encountered him, he profusely apologized and told me that what he had done was improper, and he would never do it again. I accepted his apology, and the incident was never mentioned thereafter.

Figure 21. Staircase leading up to the Clock Tower in Graz, where I would often sit and study on the benches in the alcoves.

A Hunger Game

While I was enrolled in business college in Graz, I lost 20 pounds by the end of my first year. Food was still a very scarce commodity, and I could never find enough to eat. Barter was the only other option, but this was only possible when one had clothing, jewelry, or different food to exchange. Most ordinary citizens had no such advantage, so many people had no choice but to endure a starvation diet for an extended period of time.

While attending college, I was boarding with an elderly widow. Despite my father paying her plenty for my keep, she kept most of the food for herself, willfully depriving me of even basic rations. She didn't seem to care that on many days I had nothing to eat but a cold potato and a leaf of lettuce. As soon as my father saw what was going on, he moved me into another apartment, where I started to cook for myself with food provided by my father.

All of this misery was still the direct aftermath of the war. Nazi Germany had regarded Austria as a constituent part of the German state, but in 1943 the Allies agreed in the Moscow Declaration (or "Declaration of the Four Nations on General Security") that Austria was the first victim of Nazi aggression, and thus would be treated as an independent and liberated country after the war was over. Even so, the Allied occupation lasted for ten years, from 1945-1955.

During this time, Austria, like Germany, was divided into four occupation zones or sectors, each held by the United States, United Kingdom, Soviet Union, and France, respectively. The city of Vienna, like Berlin, was similarly subdivided, with a central district administered jointly by the Allied Control Council.

While helping my father to sell electric motors and farming equipment at a Viennese exhibition in 1951, I met Leopold Figl, who was Chancellor of Austria from 1945-1953. He shook hands with my father and showed an interest in the equipment, as he was an expert in agriculture. Chancellor Figl had been deported to Dachau concentration camp in 1938 because he was part of the *Heimwehr* or Homeguard, the Austrian resistance opposed to the Nazi takeover. In 1943 he was released to work as an oil engineer, but was rearrested in 1944 and taken to Mauthausen concentration camp. In February 1945, he was sentenced to death for "high treason" in Vienna, but narrowly escaped as the execution had not yet been carried out by the end of the war.

Despite many hardships, I graduated with honors from business college in 1948 and was immediately offered a job by the Chamber of Commerce in Graz. But my family needed me, so I had to go home; in the meantime, my father had started a new business and hoped that my education would help him in making the venture a success, as living conditions in Austria were still very poor and desperate until about 1950, when the country finally began to recover.

Figure 22. Austrian Chancellor Leopold Figl.

Part Two: Seeing the World

Figure 23. The Abbey of Santa Maria de Montserrat, in Catalonia, Spain.

Maria Rosa

Royal Pains in London

When I was 18, I grew impatient with my limited life in Austria and felt that I needed to broaden my horizons. I decided to leave for England in order to improve my English language skills. By then, I had acquired six years of school English, and had conversed extensively with several English-speaking people. I was therefore quite confident of my ability to understand and adapt to the language.

My timing was poor, however: I crossed the English Channel during wintertime, and the stormy weather made the sea churn wildly. The ferry bounced up and down so violently that I felt seasick for three days afterward.

I took the train to London, where I stayed with a family living in West Kensington who had hired me, through a job agency, to care for their one-year-old baby girl. The lady of the house was pregnant, and her husband was absent most of the time, as his work was located on the Portuguese island of Madeira. He would come home once a month at most, and carried the title of "Esquire," so I believe he was a member of the British nobility, with a very responsible position on the island.

The household consisted of a relatively small apartment in a high-rise building, with no more than 1200 square feet in total. There were two bedrooms, one small living room, a kitchen, and a bathroom. The building had an elevator, and everything looked fairly new, but the apartment always felt stuffy and cramped.

Once in London, I soon found out that I was really quite mistaken about my fluency in English. I found it very difficult to understand many of the various

British accents, let alone quickly adopting them into my own speech. With many people I struggled to converse or even make myself understood.

I shared the tiny second bedroom with the one-year-old girl; I had no room of my own, and my official position was only that of "babysitter." However, my duties were often more extensive and demanding than this job title would imply.

I understand now, since the pregnant mother's husband was gone most of the time on his job, that she needed some company. But I could not understand the daily routine she enforced upon me: every morning, no matter whether it was cold, foggy, or raining, I was required to dress the baby and get her ready to go out by nine o'clock. Of course, I had to wake up very early to accomplish this task on time. Then I was expected to put the little girl in the baby buggy and take a long walk with her, pushing the stroller in front of me.

Despite the arduous routine and poor weather, my walks in West Kensington were usually quite pleasant, as this was an extremely nice and upscale part of London – although I wasn't truly conscious of the area's significance at the time. I would walk regularly to Hyde Park or St. James Park – little did I realize these are two of the famous "Royal Parks of London"! I would spend an hour or two there each time, strolling by the ponds with the baby and feeding the ducks or other waterfowl from the public birdfeeder. I was not familiar with the geography of the city, so I was also not aware that these areas were often frequented by nobility who lived nearby.

This was my daily routine, even when it was pouring cats and dogs outside. I was not permitted to return home to the apartment until about one o'clock in the afternoon, although the lady of the house would never tell me why that was. Perhaps she simply wanted a few more hours of sleep without being disturbed.

Along with supervising the child, my other chores included vacuuming the front room and some cleaning here and there. My host would not let me use her kitchen however – she didn't like my cooking, and usually insisted on frying fish every day. There was apparently very little food in the house, and even less for me.

I received only two shillings a week for my wages. Such a small sum was a pittance, given the countless hours I dedicated to her and her baby. My only days off were Wednesday afternoons, from about two o'clock onward, and I was required to be home again by midnight.

I soon became familiar with Hammersmith Palais, a dancehall and entertainment venue within walking distance, where young people met, danced, and enjoyed trendy music from different bands playing there each week. I did meet some nice people, but I was still very young and inexperienced, and had no money, so I never attempted to cultivate any sort of social life. I was much more interested in the music – especially this new contemporary music that was being played in England. It was just so much livelier than what I heard back in Austria! And of course, I wanted to learn better English, whether it was through books, songs, or conversation.

During my walks I came across a tea shop, where I would buy some hot tea and a finger sandwich with my two shillings each Wednesday. That was always the highlight of my week, for the entire duration of my stay in London. This snack would have to last me till midnight, or even the next day.

Given my pathetic wages and the lack of food in the house, I had very little to eat most of the time. I lost 20 pounds within 3-4 months and was suffering from malnutrition. My hair was beginning to dry up and fall out. And yet, each morning when I walked out with the baby, my host would hand me two grapes to feed the girl. How odd, I thought. I had never seen any grapes in the kitchen, so I wondered where she hid them from me. Never would she offer me even one single grape!

One might have figured that the lady was poor, but hardly: every week she came home from shopping with a bag full of brand new toddler clothes. These were expensive 4-piece winter outfits that her little girl was still much too small to be able to wear. She collected these as if she were slightly obsessed. Her odd behavior defied explanation in my young and inexperienced mind.

Figure 24. Hammersmith Palais in London.

The Beefeaters

During my long walks through this posh area of London, I passed by many famous landmarks, including Kensington Gardens – once the private gardens of Kensington Palace, the official residence of the British Royal Family since the 17th century. Speaking of royalty, I also enjoyed viewing the stately Buckingham Palace, the official residence and principal workplace of the British monarch, who was then King George VI. Strolling down nearby Piccadilly Street, I would see many street artists drawing with colorful chalk, most of them being students from the Royal Academy of Arts practicing their technique or even showing off their skills, with a low-budget yet trendy medium.

Figure 25. Royal Foot Guards with their bearskin hats.

To Hell and Back

Another common sight in London were the various members of the Royal Guard in their bright, eye-catching uniforms. Most popular were perhaps the Yeomen Warders, known colloquially as the Beefeaters. These are the ceremonial guardians of the Tower of London, a historic castle prison on the north bank of the River Thames, and were traditionally appointed to safeguard the British Royal Crown Jewels and look after any prisoners in the Tower. In practice, they commonly act as tour guides, and are certainly a tourist attraction in their own right. The Yeomen Warders are often confused with another distinct corps, the Yeomen of the Guard, who are the official Royal Bodyguards of the British monarch. The Beefeaters may have gotten their name from the Yeomen of the Guards' privilege of eating as much beef as they desired from the King's table.

Other infantry and cavalry regiments from the King's Guard (or Queen's Guard, as the case may be), are charged with guarding the official royal residences in London. As such, they were also appointed as sentries outside Buckingham Palace, watching and patrolling day and night.

Certain Foot Guard units, such as the Irish Guards and Welsh Guards, usually wore their bright red uniforms with distinctive tall fur caps, known as bearskins. The standard bearskins of the British Foot Guard are still made of genuine fur, harvested every year from an annual cull of Canadian black and brown bears by native Inuit hunters, as part of a government-run program to keep wild bear populations in check.

On Horse Guards Road, near the entrance to the Horse Guards building, I encountered of course the Horse Guards - a mounted cavalry unit also known as the King's (or Queen's) Life Guard. Horse Guards Road is the official main entrance to Buckingham

Figure 26. Yeomen Warder or Beefeater at the Tower of London.

Palace, and as such, sentries are also posted there daily. The road runs adjacent to a large courtyard or parade ground known as Horse Guards Parade, the site for the annual ceremony of "Trooping the Colour," which commemorates the official birthday of the King or Queen, as well as other precision drills involving horses, cannons, music, and fireworks.

All these various Guards and Beefeaters were such a ubiquitous fixture during my stay in London that I started to take them for granted, even though they were quite an impressive sight, along with the many historical buildings and beautifully manicured gardens.

Figure 27. Royal Horse Guards (Queen's Life Guard) at Horse Guards Parade.

Churchill's Island

As I mentioned previously, the lady's husband came home at most once a month, for only a few days or a long weekend. The rest of the time, he was occupied with his job on the island of Madeira. He never told me what his work actually was, but due to his title of Esquire, I presumed he was either a banker or an attorney. His last name originated with English nobility.

Madeira is located in the North Atlantic Ocean just above the Canary Islands, and is now the outermost region of the European Union. The island has long been a popular year-round vacation resort, now being visited by about one million tourists annually. Madeira is noted for its wine, flowers, scenic landscapes, and embroidery artisans, as well as New Year celebrations which feature the largest fireworks show in the world. The island was at this time a Portuguese possession, but was granted political autonomy in 1976.

Winston Churchill, Prime Minister of the United Kingdom from 1940-45, also spent his holidays on Madeira. He considered the island a special retreat and was particularly fond of the Reid's Palace hotel in the capital of Funchal, where he worked on his paintings and war memoirs.

I vividly remember the huge bunches of bananas the lady's husband brought every time he came home. This tropical fruit was still something of the exotic for me – I had only ever seen one banana in my life, the one my father gave me as a small child. Oddly, this couple took pains to hide the fruit from me as soon as I looked away, which was then to be eaten while I was out of sight.

Never did they offer me even one bite. I began to wonder if they were trying to starve me to death on purpose.

One morning as I was getting the baby ready, the husband opened his bedroom door, thinking I had already left. To my shock and surprise, he was completely naked, standing silent and immobile in his doorway. He stared across the hall as if lost deep in thought, completely unaware that I could see him, his plump body covered with thick dark hair. As he slouched over, I thought to myself that he looked just like a gorilla! I hid my face in embarrassment.

After about 3-4 months, the relationship between the wife and I was fast becoming intolerable. I was very disgruntled with the entire situation, and the lady constantly complained that she couldn't understand what I was saying and was worried that my accent would influence her child's linguistic development. So they offered to find me another job, which I agreed to.

The next morning, they took me to 10 Downing Street, the famous headquarters of Her Majesty's Government and the office of the Prime Minister. It had also been the residence and workplace of Prime Minister Winston Churchill from 1940-1945.

Needless to say, I was quite taken aback. The building seemed huge, consisting of several floors with many offices, conference and reception rooms, dining halls, as well as an intermediary service floor which Churchill later transformed into a restaurant. The husband and wife led me down into the dark and massive basement, which housed a large kitchen full of servants and senior workers.

They told me that my new duty was to work in the kitchen. The supervisor pointed to a huge pile of potatoes on the counter and expected me to stand there peeling, until the pile was gone. Now, I had little kitchen experience up till this point; I also wasn't received with the warmest welcome. The entire prospect seemed gloomy. I decided right there and then that I just wasn't willing to be a kitchen maid, as I came from a business family. So I thanked them and told them I would make preparations to go back to Austria instead.

Back in 1950, London was still very dependent on burning coal for fuel. Every time the fog rolled in, it mixed with the thick black smoke, creating a sort of suffocating smog full of particulate matter, which was extremely unhealthy for the lungs. By today's standards, it would be considered a severe air quality hazard.

I had been staying in London from January to April, going outdoors every day, and the weather had been terrible almost the entire time. I had lost a lot of weight, and did not tolerate the cold weather very well. Soon after deciding to return home, I found myself slumped over in the high-rise elevator, barely able to breathe or move. I had developed a severe case of pneumonia.

Seeing me weak and gasping for breath, the lady finally allowed me to spend my final days in London taking bed rest, rather than walking the stroller. (But she still didn't offer me any bananas.)

Figure 28. Huge bunches of bananas.

Jubilee

As soon as I recuperated enough to travel, I returned to Austria. When my mother saw me, she was horrified by how thin and frail I looked. I was still recovering from pneumonia, and my formerly thick, beautiful hair was dull and dry. I was glad to be home and wondered if I ever should have taken that trip to England. But eventually I was able to look back on my stay in London as a rich source of life experience; it helped me to grow up, learn about people, and familiarize myself with different types of English accents.

1950/51 in Austria was still not the best of times; people continued to suffer from the harsh aftermath of the war. Even so, I maintained a positive outlook on life: I've always been the type of person who looks forward to something new and better the following day - and that attitude has kept me going strong all these years.

I went back to work with my father for a couple of months, but he could tell that my health was not tolerating the cool, damp Austrian weather too well. So when he paid me my wages, he gave me a bonus and said, "Why don't you take a trip to Italy, where you can enjoy some warmth and sunshine." I loved the idea, so I made reservations for a cheap summer tour package.

My first stop was Rome and the Vatican. I was very excited to see Pope Pius XII, as 1950 had been declared a holy year of Jubilee - a year of joy and remission of sin for all who confess and visit the Basilica. The Pope also used the occasion of the 1950 Jubilee to declare a new national anthem for Vatican City.

Figure 29. St. Peter's Square and Basilica in Vatican City, Rome.

Pius XII was known for utilizing diplomacy to aid Holocaust victims, and directed his Roman Catholic Church to provide discreet aid to thousands of Jews. The Chief Rabbi of Rome, Elio Toaff, said regarding Pius, "Jews will always remember what the Catholic Church did for them by order of the Pope during the Second World War. When the war was raging, Pius spoke out very often to condemn the false race theory."

When I arrived at St. Peter's Square in Rome, a huge crowd of pilgrims had gathered to see Pope Pius as he held public Mass. My enthusiasm was soon dampened as the atmosphere was not at all what I had expected. Members of the crowd were pushing and shoving each other aggressively, making a great deal of noise, and acting in a very unruly and unholy manner. I left upset and disappointed, wondering why a seemingly sacred event had turned into a mob-like frenzy.

To Hell and Back

Figure 30. Inside the Blue Grotto sea cave, Isle of Capri.

To rest and relax, I then visited a beach resort in the Roman district of Ostia. Many bathing establishments were built on the seaside there after World War II, and the area soon became a favorite for tourists on summer holiday. I took a dip in the warm ocean waters, unaware that it was customary at the time for locals to pinch women on the buttocks. As I swam around absentmindedly, a man suddenly came up from underneath me and pinched me on my rear. AHHH! I screamed, scared out of my wits! I thought it was a shark! That was the end of my swimming.

My next stop was Naples, where I visited the huge, looming Mount Vesuvius, the infamous volcano that overlooks the city. We tourists walked a trail up to the edge of the caldera or volcanic crater, and everyone was peering over the edge with a sort of foolish and morbid fascination. Acrid smoke was billowing up, carrying a strong smell of sulfur. The stench was horrible, and looking down into the deep black crater was like staring into the pit of Hell. I thought to myself that this must be the flatulence of

Figure 31. Approaching the harbor, Isle of Capri.

the Devil himself! I couldn't get out of there fast enough.

I then visited the ruins of the city of Pompeii, which had been buried under ash by the 79 AD eruption of Mt. Vesuvius. I saw the natural plaster casts of the victims who had been charred and buried alive under hot ash and cinders in the "Garden of the Fugitives." To me, this was all very gloomy, and I decided I had had enough of death.

My final stop was the isle of Capri, to the south of Naples. The imposing white limestone cliffs were in clear view as I approached by boat. The highlight of my trip was a beautiful sea cave called the Blue Grotto. I entered the cave's low portal in a tiny rowboat. When the sunlight shines through the two openings of the cave, one can witness a unique visual phenomenon. A brilliant blue light illuminates the cavern from below, and when you stick your hand into the water it appears to glow!

On my way back to Austria, I took a short detour to Venice where I rode a gondola to the magnificent Doge's Palace - the official residence of the Doge of Venice (the supreme authority of the Republic of Venice). The building was opened to the public as a museum in 1923. Built in the Venetian Gothic style, the palace's facade was constructed from gleaming white and pink marble. Inside, the walls, ceilings, and floors are lavishly embellished with gold and ivory. Almost every room is filled with sculptures and paintings - the sheer wealth and extravagance was overwhelming!

My vacation lasted for approximately two weeks, after which I returned to Austria.

Figure 32. Doge's Palace and gondola, Venice, Italy.

Maria Rosa

Rites of Passage

From 1950-1952, my father and I worked very diligently together. He sold farming equipment, diesel motors, and electric motors to Austrian agriculturalists and businesspeople. We attended several industry exhibitions in Graz, Vienna, and Innsbruck, where I helped him in sales, marketing, and accounting. Due to my business education, I was now a very well-trained and efficient salesperson. My father had been hoping my little brother would join him as a personal assistant, but Frank was not interested in business, so I adopted that role as well.

By the summer of 1951, I had earned another two-week vacation as a reward for my industrious efforts. My father was scheduled to go fox-hunting and hang out with his local buddies at a community meetup, but I felt this was not for me, so I sought out better options. A certain Dr. M. had been advertising his various guided tours and adventure trips, so I decided to sign up for a group tour to Spain, Portugal, and Morocco to further educate myself about various countries and lifestyles that I was heretofore unfamiliar with.

I was curious about the world and still looking to find something or someplace that would truly resonate with me on a personal level. I had been writing back and forth in English to a pen-pal from Argentina who had piqued my interest in Spanish culture, so I felt this was a good opportunity to help me decide whether or not I would later visit him in South America. I was also enticed by the offer of a guided tour to India, but felt that this prospect was still a tad too exotic for me.

Figure 33. Plaza de España in Madrid, Spain.

I met Dr. M. for the first time when our group of 10 – 15 tourists assembled to depart from Austria. Short, stout, and bald, his strangely pinched facial features somehow made him resemble a rodent, I thought. But he spoke seven languages, and I knew I needed a tour guide who could properly communicate with the cultures we would encounter, so he seemed as good as any. However, after meeting him I would forever remember him as Dr. Ratty.

He immediately instructed everyone to exchange their money for American dollars, which would be readily accepted at all the locations we were about to visit. Apparently other American things were less acceptable, as when I wore a pair of slacks for the sake of ease and comfort during travel, I was abruptly hissed at by women in Madrid who seemed to think this style of clothing wasn't "feminine" or "proper" by their standards. This ultra-conservative aspect of the society considerably bothered me, but I did enjoy the

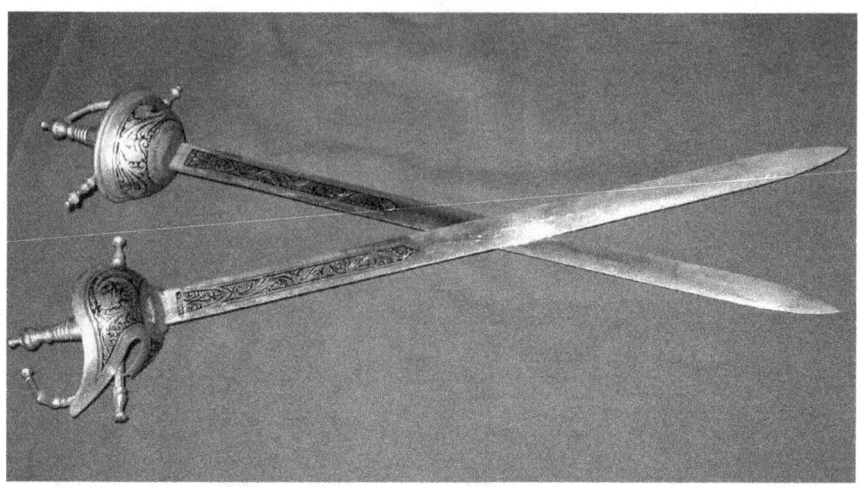

Figure 34. Antique swords from Toledo.

sight-seeing in Spain, which included many churches, cathedrals, and shops.

In Toledo, we were taken to a factory where artisans produced traditional Toledo steel swords and knives. For centuries, Toledo steel has been famous for its hardness and quality. As souvenirs, I purchased a sword as well as a dagger, the blades and hilts of both ornately decorated. We proceeded by bus to Seville in the south of Spain, where I was greatly impressed by the Moorish architecture. The cozy courtyards, tile facades, orange groves, water fountains, and geometric Arabic motifs were all very new to me, and seemed to possess a unique flavor and beauty.

We then proceeded by night to Algeciras, at the Strait of Gibraltar, where we were to cross over to Tangier, Morocco. The night was pitch black, and we were scheduled to board the 4 am ferry which would shuttle us across the Strait. The sea was extremely rough, tossing the boat rapidly back and forth. The foreign men on board appeared to be equally rough characters, so I grew very wary and afraid for my safety. The entire atmosphere during this crossing seemed eerie and threatening.

We managed to safely land in Tangier, where we boarded a train to Casablanca. The ride was long and uncomfortable, lasting several hours, during which we saw practically nothing but the sand and desert of the Western Sahara interspersed between ridges of the Atlas mountain range. The city itself, back in 1952, was quite unruly. For some reason our rat-like guide took us only to the Old Medina area, the oldest and most dilapidated quarter, and told us that we must leave again within a few hours. There was to be no dining, no hotel, and no rest, nor would we visit any of the more modern or famous landmarks.

Figure 35. Bazaar (outdoor market) in the Old Medina, Casablanca.

Figure 36. Street in 1950s Casablanca.

Instead, we walked through an outdoor bazaar with a maze of small streets, alleys, and crowded stalls. At this point in time, the Old Medina appeared unwholesome and decrepit, and was very unpleasant even in terms of a marketplace. Many men were sitting idly in the streets, smoking their pipes or hookahs, leering when young women walked by. While our tour guide appeared unusually distracted, chatting busily with locals around a dark corner, we were witness to women fighting in the middle of the street, screaming and pulling each other's hair out in what seemed to be jealous rage. I wasn't used to this sort of environment, so what I saw disturbed me deeply.

For lunch, we visited another ramshackle stall and purchased sticks of fried bread heavily spiced with cinnamon, very similar to today's Mexican churros. Dr. Ratty then sent us on an equally uncomfortable nighttime train and ferry back to Spain. In hindsight, we tourists suspected that our guide might have been conducting some nefarious activities, as his secretive behavior and rushed demeanor seemed to indicate a hidden agenda.

After returning to Spain, we stopped in Barcelona, where we visited the nearby mountain of Montserrat, the site of a famous Benedictine abbey, Santa Maria de Montserrat. The monastery hosts the sanctuary of the Virgin of Monserrat, depicted by an unusual wooden statue of a black-skinned Madonna and Child. The abbey is rumored to be the location of the Holy Grail in Arthurian myth.

Figure 37. The Benedictine abbey of Montserrat.

Figure 38. The Black Madonna statue in the sanctuary of the Virgin of Monserrat.

We then traveled on to Portugal, stopping at the capital city of Lisbon. The streets were bustling with activity, and Dr. Ratty ushered us into a familiar row of shops where everything was on sale for $1. Everyone did a lot of shopping, and I was able to buy a pair of shoes for $1.00, as well as a bottle of wine for my father for same. Of course, little Dr. Ratty never told us how much the American dollar was worth against the Portuguese currency, so for all we knew, we might have severely overpaid while financing his cohorts who were waiting with outstretched hands.

To Hell and Back

Our last stop was the famous Portuguese town of Fátima. Until 1917, Fátima had been an unknown village, centered around sheepherding and agriculture, but the small hamlet drew worldwide attention after three young shepherd children experienced a series of apparitions of the Virgin Mary between May 13th and October 13th, 1917, about one kilometer from town.

The three girls - Lúcia and her cousins, Francisco and Jacinta Marto - were guarding their sheep in Cova da Iria on May 13th, 1917 when they witnessed an apparition of a lady dressed in white. She then visited the children again on the 13th of every month through October. "Our Lady of Fátima" communicated a message to them which consisted of three secrets. According to the official interpretation of the Catholic Church, the three secrets involve Hell and redemption, World War I and World War II, and the attempted assassination of Pope John Paul II. The third secret was written down in 1943, concealed by the Church, and held privately by the Vatican from 1957-2000 until it was finally revealed to the public. Due to its highly controversial nature, accusations have been lodged against the Church for allegedly not divulging the true or full message in its original form.

The final visitation occurred on October 13th, 1917 and was witnessed by 70,000 pilgrims who witnessed the so-called Miracle of the Sun, during which many different apparitions and visual phenomena occurred.

With this said, we arrived at what looked to be a very dusty, dry, and desolate village. Our guide did not inform us that the Basilica or Sanctuary of Our Lady of Fátima, now located at the site of the visions, was still under construction though near completion; rather, he silently walked us to a "town square"-type courtyard in the sparsely populated rural area of Cova da Iria, where we sat down on benches surrounding a central fountain shaded by sparse, brittle trees. Nearby, he pointed out a dilapidated wooden icon shaped like an arch with a cross on top, which sat as a location marker for the historical events which had taken place. One dusty contemplation bench was forlornly situated beside it.

I thought to myself that if there had ever been any sacred occurrences here, it was surely not apparent now. Then we were taken to the base of the nearby hills to see the various geological formations, including rows of limestone caves and rock grottoes where monks and hermits once lived and prayed.

The hamlet with its meandering sheep and arid landscape seemed very poor and unimpressive during my visit, but the construction of the Sanctuary of Our Lady of Fátima brought much local development to the region, which eventually allowed the town of Fátima to be elevated to the status of city on July 12, 1997.

Today the spacious sanctuary at Cova da Iria, the site of the apparitions, has become the principal focus of visitors, along with numerous other churches and chapels. Annual Christian pilgrims regularly fill the country roads leading to the shrine, where numbers can swell to the hundreds of thousands during May 13th and October 13th (the dates associated with the visions). The economy of the town now relies on this large-scale religious tourism.

We returned from Portugal back to Spain, and finally to Austria. Not once did we have an opportunity to sit down for an actual meal, and for the duration of the trip we only rested in dilapidated motels for a few hours at a time. Traveling all the way down to Casablanca and back within ten days required a grueling schedule. The majority of our time was spent rushing onto busses and trains, and looking out the window for sight-seeing.

While my trip was severely lacking in many ways, and relatively expensive since it was supposed to include "full room and board," I still felt it to be a worthwhile experience, helping me to familiarize myself with geography, culture, and various cities I would otherwise know little about. However, I decided that Argentina and other Hispanic countries would most likely not be on my future itineraries.

Figure 39. Sanctuary of Our Lady of Fátima, today.

Maria Rosa

Mr. Sewermeister

I continued to work for my father the following year, and in the summer of 1952, I took another short vacation. During a brief stopover in Paris, I visited the beautiful white Sacré-Coeur (Sacred Heart) Basilica, located at the highest point of the city. The mosaic in the apse, entitled *Christ in Majesty*, is one of the largest in the world and is embellished with lustrous gold leaf.

My journey also took me past the famous Arc de Triomphe monument. 164 feet tall and 148 feet wide, the "Triumphal Arch" stands at the western end of the Champs-Élysées and honors those who fought and died for France in the French Revolutionary and Napoleonic Wars.

Beneath the Arc is the Tomb of the Unknown Solider from World War I (and now also World War II). The monument also features an eternal flame, which burns in memory of the dead soldiers who were never identified.

After its construction, the Arc de Triomphe became a rallying point for French troops parading after successful military campaigns. Following Nazi Germany's victory over Paris, German soldiers entered the city on June 14, 1940, parading down the Champs-Élysées and around the Arc de Triomphe. On August 29, 1944, during the Allied Liberation of Paris, victorious American troops marched down the Champs-Élysées with the Arc as a backdrop and warplanes flying overhead.

In 1961, President John F. Kennedy and First Lady Jacqueline Kennedy paid their respects at the Tomb of the Unknown Soldier. After the 1963 assassination of President Kennedy, Mrs. Kennedy, recollecting the eternal flame at the Arc de Triomphe, requested that an eternal flame also be placed next to her husband's grave at Arlington National Cemetery in Virginia.

Returning afterward to England, I visited several new places including Brighton, where an antiquarian pirate ship pulled into the quaint historical seaside marina. The vessel was wonderfully preserved and proved to be a fantastic tourist attraction, with many youngsters jumping around playfully, pretending to be pirates – "yo ho ho, and a bottle o' rum!"

I then visited Oxford, as I was curious about this prestigious university town that had grown so famous in academic circles. I was impressed with the city's quaint beauty and peaceful upscale communities, thinking to myself that it seemed like a particularly pleasant place to live. Oxford was and still is a very green city, and the historical architecture and vibrant parks and nature walks left an exceedingly positive impression on me.

Moving on, I decided to visit my English pen-pal and his sister in Gloucester, as they had been writing to me for years. These high-spirited youths lived with their grandparents in a dark and gloomy row house, so to break the monotony we would visit the Gloucester Cathedral and ride a motorcycle through the meadows alongside the River Severn. I enjoyed the historic architecture in this city as well, with its many gabled medieval and Tudor houses.

I then received news that I had been accepted for an appointment with the Canadian consulate for the purpose of obtaining an immigration visa, so I rushed back to Austria. I had taken this step because I was, quite frankly, at the end of my rope: my father had apprenticed me to his certified accountant, with whom I had been spending countless hours poring over ledger sheets full of cramped columns filled with tiny numbers. This repulsive old man was a heavy chain-smoker and seemed to always be in my face, criticizing and complaining. Not only did I have to put up with his incessant puffing and obnoxious demeanor, but the most disgusting odor also emanated from his mouth every time he spoke. Being next to him was just like smelling an open sewer pit, or even worse, the caldera at Mt. Vesuvius. The thought of continuing to work with him made me want to throw up.

The Canadian consulate in Austria finally accepted my Visa application. During the subsequent wait of several months for processing and review, I grit my teeth and continued to work for my father until the end of 1952. In early March of 1953, I made an appearance at a final exhibition, where my father requested the accountant's attendance, even going to the expense of paying for the man's upscale hotel room.

On the second morning of the exhibition, Mr. Sewermeister was scheduled to meet with my father at 10 am, but by noon he was still nowhere to be seen. Was he still asleep? Did something happen? My father requested that I check in on him and fetch him from the hotel if necessary.

Upon knocking on the door of the accountant's hotel suite, I received no answer. Twisting the doorknob, I found that the door was unlocked, so I stepped in. Silence. The bed appeared disheveled, so I took another couple of steps toward it.

As soon as Mr. Sewermeister heard me, he jumped out of bed unclothed. Panicking, he fished for a sheet to pull up to hide his nakedness. A slovenly, nude woman whom I had never seen before lay beside him and asked what was going on. To my knowledge, Mr. Sewermeister was unmarried.

I immediately closed the door and left, even more disgusted. After reporting the story to my father, he vowed to fire him. In March of 1953, I departed for Canada.

Figure 40. Tourists and American troops at the Arc de Triomphe, Paris.

Saturnia: Vomit on the High Seas

Shortly after receiving my immigration visa, I arrived at the busy port of Milan, Italy, scheduled to catch a passenger ship en route to Canada. I was to go aboard the *MS Saturnia*, but while waiting for boarding time to arrive I was approached by a middle-aged officer from another ocean liner docked nearby: the enormous *SS Andrea Doria*. Having just undertaken its maiden voyage in January of 1953, the vessel was a source of Italian national pride, as it was considered one of the country's largest, fastest, and supposedly safest ships during a time when Italy was still attempting to repair its economy and reputation in the wake of World War II.

Gleaming white, the shiny new *Andrea Doria* towered over us. The officer asked me if I wanted to come on board with him and "have a look around." Noticing that he seemed to be eyeing certain parts of my anatomy for a little too long, I decided it best to let him know that I wasn't interested, as I would soon be departing on another ship.

In July of 1956, the *SS Andrea Doria* took its last voyage, catastrophically colliding with a cruise ship off the coast of Massachusetts. 46 people died as a result, and the accident is still considered one of the worst maritime disasters to occur in U.S. waters. Learning of this fateful event, I felt very fortunate to have never taken this ship during my various overseas journeys.

I departed Milan as scheduled. Making its way west through the Mediterranean Sea, the *MS Saturnia* temporarily docked at other ports in Italy and Spain to collect additional passengers and supplies. As I waited through these many stopovers, impatient with the continued delays, I learned more about the unusual history of the ship.

The *Saturnia* began operations in 1932 as part of the "Italia Line" (or Italian Line), a transatlantic passenger shipping company based in Italy. This ship was one of the first liners to offer a large number of cabins with private balconies. During World War II, the *Saturnia* was captured by the United States and converted into a troopship, or troop transporter. As one of only four ships in the Italian Line to survive the war, it resumed commercial service in 1947 under a new company name and continued operating until it was scrapped in 1965.

The trip seemed endless. The weather at sea was cold and gloomy, and hundreds of immigrant passengers milled about, looking for friendship and social opportunities. Periodically, the tedium was broken by recordings of Billy Graham's evangelical sermons booming through the loudspeakers. I had never heard anything like this before, and his strong charismatic preacher's voice and powerful messages held me spellbound. At the time, I was not aware that Billy Graham was regarded as a spiritual adviser to several U.S. Presidents including Dwight D. Eisenhower, and later, Lyndon Johnson and Richard Nixon.

The cuisine on board was, expectedly, traditional Italian. While the daily pasta and tomato sauce was at first quite appetizing, it soon became very monotonous. To make matters worse, the kitchen was extremely fond of using copious amounts of seemingly over-ripe parmesan cheese which, mixed with the aroma of the tomato sauce, began to produce an odor that decidedly reminded me of stale vomit.

By the end of the first week, the rancid, odiferous stench had grown so oppressive that it automatically turned my stomach and induced me to involuntarily throw up. For the remaining week of the journey, I would struggle to eat and keep my food down without gagging.

Figure 41. The *Saturnia*.

Part Three: Adventures in Canada and Abroad

Figure 42. Hotel Embassy, Broadway, New York City.

Maria Rosa

The End of the World

The *Saturnia* arrived at the port of Halifax, Nova Scotia at the end of March 1953, at 3 o'clock in the morning. The night was very dark and cold. Glancing ahead as we neared the shore, the only thing I could see at first was the pale beam of a distant lighthouse. I wondered if we had reached the end of the world – would the ship momentarily sail over the edge and tumble into the dark abyss?

After I landed on the moon – ahem, excuse me, after I disembarked in this unearthly and forlorn nighttime city, I was processed through customs and my passport was stamped by immigrations officials. I then boarded a train waiting to take me west shortly after sunrise. Several other immigrants from the ship crowded onto the train with me, and told me they were traveling in the same direction. They were from many different countries, including Italy, Austria, and Germany. All were looking for work opportunities in Canada.

After traveling all day and night by railroad, sleeping intermittently on my cramped, rigid wooden bench next to four other exhausted passengers, I arrived the next morning in Montreal, Quebec. Because the train would be pausing for a stopover of several hours, I decided to venture a brief sight-seeing foray, not knowing what to expect.

Soon, I began to feel very uncomfortable in Montreal, as it became clear to me that no one I encountered spoke any English; even worse, the locals seemed to regard me as of little worth, since I could not understand one word of French. To them, French was a language of national pride and identity, and anyone who couldn't speak it might as well not exist.

To Hell and Back

I distinctly looked forward to continuing my journey onward to a province that spoke English.

Later that evening, I again boarded the transcontinental train, running from the eastern city of Halifax to Vancouver on the west coast. Stopovers were scheduled at every larger city along the way, including Sudbury, Ontario, where I had a job waiting for me - as well as a few pen-pal acquaintances, originally from Graz, to whom I had been writing.

Figure 43. Train on the North Shore of Lake Superior.

Peaches and Ice

The journey by rail seemed endless. I had left Austria with only enough money for minimal food and my first month's rent deposit. On the side, I kept an extra $300 hidden, which I held onto for dear life in case I needed to buy a ticket back to Austria by ship. Under no other circumstances would I touch these funds.

I slept in my seat, then purchased a small meal when we arrived in Ottawa, the Canadian capital. The next day, I stepped off the train in Sudbury and proceeded to meet my pen-pals. Sudbury is located in northern Ontario, on the Canadian side of the Great Lakes, close to Sault Ste. Marie and North Bay.

Within one week, I secured a nice room from an elderly lady for $10 a week in a relatively fancy home, and started my new office job with a Canadian import firm. By now, my English had improved, enabling me to understand and communicate well enough to perform my office duties efficiently. Nevertheless, the early "spring" weather was very challenging for me to endure: it was extremely cold. I had never experienced such bone-chilling cold in my life. Although I had brought a heavy coat with me, I had no slacks; I only wore stockings, which was a huge mistake - I felt like my legs were going to freeze the very first week! Every day, I shivered on my way to and from my place of employment. Hot tea became my lifeline.

In spite of the cold, I stayed in Sudbury for almost a year. In that city, I never experienced any animosity toward foreigners whatsoever. People were very kind and friendly, and I enjoyed socializing as much as I could, although I was usually busy working in the import firm's bookkeeping department. My wages were fair but not great – just enough to sustain myself.

My employer's main import was fresh fruit and vegetables from California, which he resold to Canadian distributors. At one point, my boss found himself with a surplus of peaches and avocados, and offered them to his employees at a discount. I had no idea what an avocado was at this time, but the peaches sure looked appealing. I went ahead and bought myself a whole lug of them at a clearance price, and took them back to my room.

Attempting to save money, I ate almost nothing but peaches for several days in a row. By the end of the week, I came down with the worst case of hives. I then decided I needed to find a local grocery store where I could shop properly on a budget.

Christmas in Sudbury that year was my favorite and most positive experience in Canada – everyone was so congenial and hospitable, treating me like one of their family. The memory leaves me warm-hearted even today.

Figure 44. The Dionne Quintuplets.

Maria Rosa

The Ontario Quintuplets

By the summer of 1953, at the age of 21, I had already made many friends and acquaintances in Sudbury. One day, I was introduced to a young couple by the name of Ernie and Jeanette. They seemed like very friendly people, classy and attractive, and were driving an unusually nice car. The couple invited me on a trip to Corbeil, which was a village north of Sudbury and Sault Ste. Marie, close to North Bay.

Before taking me out to a nice dinner, they drove us by a large and lavish house, a veritable mansion, made of light-colored "yellow" brick. Ernie told me that this is where the "famous Dionne quintuplets" and their family had been living. At the time, I didn't know the history of the family, nor did I have any idea even of who they were or why they were famous; but later on, I found out by coincidence from my friends that Ernie was the eldest brother of the Dionne children. Ernest was born in 1926, making him 27 at this time. He married his wife Jeanette in 1947, at the age of 20. She was a schoolteacher in Corbeil.

The Dionnes were a farming family descended from Zacharie Cloutier, a French carpenter who immigrated to Canada in the 1600s and founded one of the foremost families of Quebec. Celebrity singer Celine Dion is a descendent of the same family. After Ernie, the Dionnes had five more children, and then gave birth to the quintuplets – quite a phenomenon at the time, as they were the first quintuplets known to survive infancy, even though they were born two months premature. Their mother Elzire suspected she was carrying twins, but no one realized that quintuplets were even possible!

Four months after their birth, the Ontario government intervened and determined that the parents were unfit for the enormous task of raising the quintuplets. Custody of the five babies was withdrawn, originally for a guardianship of two years. The stated reason for removing the quintuplets from the parents' legal custody was to ensure their survival. However, the government soon realized that the sisters attracted massive public interest, so the babies were made wards of the King (or Provincial Crown of the British Commonwealth) for the next nine years, under the *Dionne Quintuplets' Guardianship Act* of 1935.

The government fostered and encouraged the tourist industry around the children, and they fast became Ontario's biggest attraction, bringing in millions of dollars in revenue and 3,000,000 visitors in total. The sisters and their likenesses were also used to market and publicize many commercial products. As a result, the government, the family, and those otherwise involved with the children profited greatly. The quintuplets also starred in two Hollywood feature films, which were essentially fictionalized versions of their story - *The Country Doctor* (1936) and *Five of a Kind* (1938).

In 1943, the Dionne parents won back custody of their children, and the entire family moved into the newly-built mansion Ernie showed me, which was paid for out of the quintuplets' fund. The quintuplets left the family home in 1952, upon turning 18 years old - only one year before I visited. After this, they had little contact with their parents.

Maria Rosa

One of the sisters, Émilie, devoted her life to becoming a nun, but experienced a series of seizures in the convent at the age of 20. She had asked not to be left unattended, but the nun who was assigned to watch Émilie assumed her to be asleep, and left to attend Mass. Émilie then had another seizure, rolled face-down onto her pillow, and unable to raise herself, suffocated.

Sadly, according to the published accounts of the surviving sisters, their parents at home had no regard or sensitivity for them as individuals, but rather treated them like a five-part unit. They were frequently lectured about the trouble they had caused the family, and much guilt was piled on them for even existing. They were strictly disciplined and punished, as well as physically abused, and often denied privileges which their other siblings received. The sisters were also unaware for many years that the lavish mansion, gourmet food, and series of luxury cars the family enjoyed were paid for with the money earned by the sisters themselves.

Although I never actually met the quintuplets, I did meet Ernie and his wife several times in Sudbury, and once again in North Bay. At the time, I still didn't realize the significance of the Dionne quintuplets. I found out later on that Ernie became a stationary engineer in North Bay, and eventually took over management of the family farm and holdings when his father died.

Where's the Beef?

I stayed in Sudbury throughout that year, until next spring. By April of 1954, I had decided that this city was just too cold for me. I suffered from many weather-related colds, and money was tight. Half of my paycheck had to go towards rent, so splurging on food was out of the question. Hoping for better prospects, I bought myself a railroad ticket to the city of Windsor in the south of Ontario.

Arriving in Windsor, I took a brief tour by bus. The weather was still biting cold, and the overall atmosphere of the city made me feel very uncomfortable. Without a visa, I was unable to cross the river into Detroit, Michigan. Railroad fares in the 1950s were still relatively inexpensive, so I bought myself another train ticket west to Vancouver, British Columbia.

Within a couple days or so, my train made a two-hour stopover in Calgary, Alberta. I was starving, so I briefly left the station to find some lunch at a nearby restaurant. Carefully watching my budget, I ordered a low-priced ham sandwich, according to the menu. Hungrily taking a bite without looking into the sandwich, I was shocked as my mouth was filled with an intensely salty, greasy, horrible-tasting mess. What the heck was this, I thought. I ordered ham!

Upon opening the sandwich and peering between the bread, I saw that the inside was filled with salt pork, rather than ham. Now, ham required some degree of refrigeration, while salt pork did not, so I wondered if this restaurant was attempting to operate without refrigeration. Were they really this foolish, or was I rather in such a forlorn outback-style pioneer outpost?

Perhaps I should have ordered a roast beef sandwich instead: Calgary at this time found itself at the center of an Alberta oil boom, and was (and still is) famous for its annual Calgary Stampede – a rodeo and festival featuring bull riding, steer wrestling, and bronco riding, as well as an agricultural exhibition. Calgarians took great pride in their cattle, and beef was a key part of the local economy.

Given the above, sometimes I giggle to myself and wonder if the chef merely wanted to spite me for ordering ham in beef-loving Calgary, only months before the Stampede!

Figure 45. Salt pork.

Cat's Soup

I arrived in Vancouver in late April, 1954. Before departing Sudbury, I had made sure to obtain a shining recommendation letter from my employer. The same agricultural import firm also had a branch in Vancouver, so I immediately applied there for a similar job. The hiring office informed me that they were impressed by my qualifications, but there was currently no opening for my specific position; however, they would "keep me posted."

In the meantime, I sought out a room for myself. Many attractive family homes displayed signs in their front yards reading "Room for Rent" – apparently numerous homeowners were in need of extra cash. Due to the competitive market, I was easily able to obtain a comfortable room in a nice house with a friendly landlord, at a lower price than what I had been paying in Sudbury.

After two days, the import firm called me back and informed me that they did indeed have a new opening for me, and I could begin work the next day. What luck! I thought. Things were really looking up!

Over the next few months, I attempted to gradually acculturate myself more to the Canadian lifestyle. Many features were still unfamiliar to me. When a friend invited me out to a local café, he ordered a plate of chips – British for French fries. I saw him grab a big bottle labeled "Catsup" and squirt the red stuff onto a corner of his plate. Mystified, I wondered to myself for a long time what this strange substance was. Catsup? Cat soup? Cats up?

....Cat supper?

Maria Rosa

I was too embarrassed to ask. It was only years later, upon encountering American "Ketchup," that I came to understand this was a tomato-based condiment that I had never seen in Europe.

When my employer offered discount-price California avocados to his office staff, my Japanese co-worker brought one to lunch every day and slurped it up with pleasure. I had no idea what these strange soft green fruits were; the word "avocado" wasn't even in my vocabulary. Not until encountering avocados once again in an American supermarket would I discover the pleasures of guacamole or avocado sushi.

I kept in touch with my parents all this time, and by summer my father was begging me to come home, telling me "I desperately need you for exhibitions. I promise things are going to get better. I promise! I'll even get rid of Mr. Sewermeister. Just come home!" Around September, he positively insisted that I come back to Austria, as he wasn't feeling well. At the same time, he sent me a ticket for another Atlantic voyage on the parmesan-laden Saturnia. I wasn't so sure this was right for me, but my conscience wouldn't let me stay in Canada.

Figure 46. What is catsup?

The Freemason's Shrine

Before leaving Vancouver to return to my father's home and business in Austria, I went to the Canadian consulate and got myself a return visa, just in case I would need it. My apprehensions about returning to Austria were still strong. Since the *Saturnia* would be departing from New York City rather than Halifax, I also obtained a visitor's visa to the United States. I was excited at the thought – I had heard so much about the USA my entire life, and now I would finally have a chance to experience a small part of this legendary nation firsthand!

The long and wearisome cross-continental train ride from Vancouver to New York paused for a brief stopover in the city of Niagara Falls, where I visited its famous namesake waterfalls. As I peered across the gorge at the immense rushing torrents, listening to the roar of the whitewater cascades, I felt a bit frightened at the sheer power and magnitude of such a waterfall. Anyone caught in those currents would surely be crushed to a pulp, I thought. Little did I know that quite a few crazed, courageous souls have attempted to swim, dive, plunge, and even tightrope walk across the falls, some to their own demise!

Moving on to New York City, I met up with some acquaintances who were recommended to me by one of my closest friends while I was still living in Austria. They were a senior couple in their 70s, husband and wife, the man being my friend's brother. I had been casually corresponding with them for the past couple of years, so they were already familiar with my situation and assured me they were happy to have visitors.

Maria Rosa

I checked into a hotel across the street from their cozy upscale Manhattan apartment. They were joyfully delighted to see me, and immediately invited me into their apartment for a cheerful lunch, letting me know I was welcome any time. The old lady was like a mother to me, and the old man was extremely charming.

At one point during my stay, the husband told me with a smile that he wanted to show me something special. He put on a conical hat with a tassel, called a fez. Then he opened the door to a large private room with unusual décor: it appeared to be some sort of shrine, with an altar, candle stands, banners, chairs, and unfamiliar symbols and emblems all around. The colorful facility appeared very regal and impressive to me, but I couldn't quite understand exactly what I was viewing. I smiled and thanked him, but I was too shy to ask questions.

I found out, later on, that he was trying to tell me he was a Freemason, as well as a member of the Shriners - a Masonic fraternity now well-known for their non-profit children's hospitals. This ornate shrine was probably a meeting place for his local Lodge. As a fraternal organization, Freemasonry now exists In various forms throughout the world, and is designed to teach morality, ethics, virtue, and brotherhood beyond the bounds of religious and racial differences, while still professing belief in a Supreme Being.

At the time, I knew absolutely nothing about Freemasonry; I didn't even know that it existed - or that my favorite composer, Wolfgang Amadeus Mozart, was himself the most famous of the Austrian Masons. I didn't know that many of the founding fathers of the United States, including George Washington and Benjamin Franklin, as well as many of the signers of the Declaration of Independence and

To Hell and Back

U.S. Constitution, were Freemasons. I did not know that many Freemasons were stilled actively involved in government, law enforcement, civil service, and charity, and actively networked to achieve many different civic goals without partisan politics.

Today, I regret that I did not have more of an opportunity to familiarize myself with the friendly and gracious people who belonged to this organization, who were so welcoming to me.

Figure 47. The Shriner.

The Mayor's Tour

While waiting for the *Saturnia Vomitus Oceanus* to dock, I stayed in Manhattan for two weeks, with the sweet elderly couple treating me like a princess the entire time. Their rooms were part of an attractive Midtown apartment complex constructed with large stone blocks, centrally located within walking distance of Times Square. Looking back now, I realize that these were Masonic apartments, and the courtly, spacious shrine room was probably shared by an entire community of Masons who lived and socialized in that building.

During the long days in waiting, I mostly passed my time in urban exploration, curiously walking up and down the crowded streets that grid the island. I would often walk down Broadway to visit Times Square, while having little cognizance of its famous reputation or significance. I also began to familiarize myself with the various boroughs and ethnic communities that constitute the massive and diverse city of New York.

Taking a stroll further down Broadway, I eventually passed the gigantic 102-story Empire State Building on foot. Walking north up Madison Avenue, I arrived at the historical St. Patrick's Cathedral, with its ornate Gothic Revival architecture and colorful stained glass windows. Curious, I went inside to view the interior. While duly impressed with its elegant arched columns and ribbed vault, as well as the beauty of the copious stained glass embellishing every wall, I was rather disappointed with the relative lack of other art within the cathedral, in comparison to what I had become familiar with in the *Stephansdom* of Vienna. In style and execution, these

Figure 48. St. Patrick's Cathedral and Atlas statue.

two cathedrals were very different from one another, and I felt a twinge of longing to visit St. Stephen's once again.

Right across from St. Patrick's Cathedral is the famous Rockefeller Center and Plaza, a complex of 19 commercial buildings covering 22 acres. At street level, about 200 flagpoles line the plaza, where flags of United Nations member counties, U.S. states and territories, as well as other motifs are flown. The plaza also features a number of unique works of art.

I couldn't help but glance upward at the distinctive GE Building (then called the RCA Building), an art deco skyscraper that forms the centerpiece of Rockefeller Center. Above the main entrance was a unique frieze by sculptor Lee Lawrie, depicting "Wisdom" – a powerful and stately bearded figure who, as I now understand, represents the "Architect," or Supreme Being of the Freemasons. He holds a golden Masonic compass in his hand, with which he

Figure 49. Lee Lawrie's Wisdom at Rockefeller Center.

traces out his cosmic designs. Below him is a quote from Isaiah 33:6, "Wisdom and Knowledge shall be the stability of thy times." Lawrie also created the famous 45-foot-tall bronze statue of Atlas that sits in front of Rockefeller Center, right across from the Cathedral. Walking further, I even reached the UN Headquarters, where I saw the flagpoles of the member nations.

One day, the elderly Freemason who hosted me was visited by one of his closest friends and associates: the mayor of a large city in New Jersey. This man also appeared to be a Mason, and was familiar with the local Lodge and apartments. The Mayor told us he would be happy to take us all on a sight-seeing tour of the areas to the south, including his home state. I jumped at the opportunity!

So that weekend, we piled into his car and drove south in the morning through Lower Manhattan and Brooklyn, all the way down to Coney Island, where we stopped for a nice lunch. However, after seeing the giant Wiener Riesenrad Ferris wheel back in Vienna, these amusement park contraptions failed to impress me. Wurstelprater Park in the Viennese district of Leopoldstadt dates back to the time of Austrian Emperor Josef II, who opened his Imperial hunting grounds to the public in 1766, which were soon built up into a sprawling public amusement center.

Resuming our journey, we crossed the Hudson River by bridge to Staten Island. Continuing our sightseeing, we then travelled north to Jersey City, New Jersey, where we eventually crossed back over to Manhattan. We managed to complete this entire round trip by the end of the day.

I was very fond of the elderly Masonic couple, and it was mutual; they showered me with small gifts and paid for scrumptious meals. They had no children of

Figure 50. United Nations Headquarters & Manhattan skyline.

To Hell and Back

their own, so to this very day I truly feel they were trying to "adopt" me! They told me that I would do well to enroll at Columbia University in Upper Manhattan, and they would make sure I was well taken care of. I pondered the idea with enthusiasm and decided to visit the Ivy League campus by bus. On the way north, the driver took us through the area of Harlem, which during the 1920s and 30s was the focus of the "Harlem Renaissance," an artistic and creative outpouring without precedent in the African-American community. However, due to the job losses of the Great Depression and the deindustrialization of New York City after World War II, crime rates and poverty had increased significantly by the time I visited. The crisis was evident in the atmosphere and even the streets, which were poorly maintained.

I was charmed by the Columbia University campus and sincerely considered staying in Manhattan for a longer period of time. But I really had no choice but to board the Saturnia once again to return to my family in Austria, and for this reason the elderly Mason and his wife were very sad. When I visited his sister again in Graz to deliver some presents, I keenly described my adventures in New York and told her all about her brother's recent life and circumstances. My report apparently made her very happy.

Figure 51. Greetings from the United Nations, New York City!

Maria Rosa

My First Love

Bidding my friends goodbye, I reluctantly boarded the *Saturnia* and departed New York City enroute to Milan, Italy. The second day after my departure, as I was taking a leisurely walk around deck, I bumped into a tall and very handsome young man.

All smiles, he extended a polite and friendly handshake greeting. This unanticipated meeting was strangely serendipitous: Mario, a strapping Italian gentleman, told me that he and his family were from Sudbury, Ontario! Feeling strangely at ease with one another, we immediately struck up a pleasant conversation about his hometown and future plans.

Mario was currently a medical student at the University of Padua in Italy, to where he was presently headed for his final year of study. During our two weeks on the ship, traveling across the Atlantic and Mediterranean, we spent many cheerful hours together, chatting and reminiscing about our lives and travels. We talked a great deal about Sudbury, where he planned to open an office, and we discovered that we had much in common.

Over time, as we cultivated a sweet and amicable friendship, we slowly began to fall in love with each other. He was always perfectly polite and gentlemanly; our companionship was simple and chaste, innocent, yet mutually enthralling. I was so captivated by our discussions that I even forgot the reek of the over-ripe parmesan wafting daily from the kitchen! When our ship stopped over in Ceuta, an autonomous Spanish city on the north coast of Africa bordering Morocco, we had a wonderful time together, taking an idyllic romantic walk by the scenic harbor as a warm breeze rustled the palm

To Hell and Back

Figure 52. Departing Manhattan.

trees above us. Later that night, we attended a lively traditional flamenco folk dance performance.

During another stopover in Algiers, Algeria, we were sitting side-by-side on a bench near a beautiful historic mosque. In a similarly friendly manner, he began to put his arm around my shoulders for the first time. But before he could even complete the gesture, a piercing, ear-splitting whistle blasted from directly behind us. Utterly startled, we hurriedly jumped up in panic, only to see that it was the Islamic police who had reprimanded us! Apparently even this innocent gesture was not permitted in public under Muslim law, at least in this city. Needless to say, we quickly left the scene in shock and embarrassment.

By the time Mario and I arrived at the port of Milan, I felt that ours was truly an honest and genuine relationship that could lead to something great. I eagerly invited him to dinner with my family, who were waiting at the harbor. My father was very pleased and ordered an extravagant seafood feast; the fish was served on a huge platter, around which mounds of large, delicious shrimp were decoratively arranged. I have never again eaten such delectable seafood as I did in Milan that night. Mario and I were in heaven!

Unfortunately, Mario's next semester in university would have to take priority over any other wishes. He told us he had to be on his way to Padua the next morning, but would very much like to see us again. My father, acting as a kind and generous host, invited Mario to our family home to spend the Christmas holiday.

I was delighted, yet I was also left with a slight apprehension as I pondered what might ensue when that time came to pass – would my brother be so welcoming? Frank has always had an unsociable side which tends to come out at the most inopportune moments, I pondered to myself...

Figure 53. Palm Trees in Ceuta.

A Slap in the Face

Starting in the fall of 1954, I resumed working for my father. I helped out at more exhibitions, saving all of my earnings. But it soon became apparent to me that this unsatisfactory routine was holding me back from my long-term ambitions.

My father had "promised things would change," but nothing had really changed at all; he was still actively hiring Mr. Sewermeister – whom he nevertheless tried to keep at a distance when I was around – and family relations were still tense. Unhappy and frustrated, I weighed my options over the course of the passing months.

As Christmas time approached, I waited in nervous anticipation for Mario to arrive. He was the one bright spot and ray of hope in my life; I even considered the prospect of returning to Sudbury with him after his graduation from medical school. Who knew what the future could hold?

In the upper floor of my parent's house, we prepared a clean guest bedroom for Mario. Adjacent to his room was my own upstairs bedroom. The night before his scheduled visit, a winter storm suddenly rolled in and dropped a heavy layer of snow. I worried, wondering if he would be able to make the journey.

The air was freezing cold, and the old stove furnaces were inadequate for heating the entirety of the house. So much for a "warm welcome": the single upstairs furnace was located in my room, and hardly any of the heated air reached Mario's quarters. For the next several days, he would struggle to stay warm.

Perhaps one might think such circumstances would have been perfect reason to invite Mario to stay in my room with me instead. After all, I knew I would have been safe with him. Unfortunately, my emotionally unstable brother did everything in his power to prevent Mario and I from spending any time together; he practically camped out in my room and wouldn't leave, neither day nor night; and when I tried to walk into Mario's room, Frank would follow me right in.

Although my brother had a poor grasp of English, he would interrupt Mario with erratic fits and utter stupidity whenever he would converse; at his worst, Frank would even spew obscene language in front of both of us. To top it off, when I wasn't present, Frank attempted to tell disparaging lies about me.

Clearly, my brother did his utmost to destroy the relationship between Mario and me. He ultimately accomplished his goal; four months had passed since the last time we spoke in Milan, and now we were given absolutely no opportunity to reignite our emotional bond, or to even get to know each other again. Rather than enjoying a pleasant vacation, each day was filled with stress and apprehension as to what kind of stunt Frank would next pull.

By New Year's Day, Mario was forced to say his goodbyes, and I was far too embarrassed and dejected to even ask about seeing him again in Sudbury. That night, he slipped away, never to return.

Over the next few months my father was frequently gone, taking care of business concerns. Although he did have a heart condition, his health had improved, and he seemed to have less need for my help. The situation at home with my brother and mother had grown palpably strained and was near the breaking point.

One day I was standing outside the house, talking casually with three friends from my father's exhibitions, including one business lady and a young British man who spoke to me in English. Suddenly, my mother came storming out the front door, screaming "Stupid bitch!" at me. In shock, I turned around, and she slapped me square and hard across the face, right in front of my friends. Words cannot describe the emotions that ran through me, nor could I fathom what my mother seemed to be assuming about me in this moment.

This cruel act of public humiliation was the straw that broke the camel's back. I decided right then and there this was not what I wanted in life. In spite of loving my family, and trying to help them in every way possible, I still felt like I was treated as an orphan, or worse, a slave.

My mother must have sensed my bitterness, as a couple days later she told me, "You better leave. You don't have anything here." I have never been able to figure out if she said this in the sincere hope that I would find something better for myself, or if she really just wanted to get rid of me as soon as possible. I do know that she considered my brother to be her "most beloved child" – after she gave birth to him, "things got a lot better in her marriage," she said. Back then, sons were still considered to be "more valuable" than daughters, even if such prejudice remained unspoken.

Unable to endure any further disrespect from my mother and brother, I decided to return to Canada the following week. During the last couple days of my stay, my mother didn't bother to cook anymore, or even to supply me with any food. I was stuck eating nothing but some dry wafers I had on hand. With each passing day, I was more certain of the rightness of my decision.

Maria Rosa

I left Austria in the spring of 1955. My mother later told me on the phone that Father "cried for days and never forgave me."

Figure 54. Transcontinental train.

Figure 55. Lower Spiral Tunnel on the Canadian Pacific railway in British Columbia.

Dancing on Thin Ice

Leaving Austria, I embarked on another familiar voyage across the Atlantic aboard the *Saturnia Vomitorium*. As I walked around deck, I was haunted everywhere by Mario's ghost. Gagging once again from the smell of the overripe parmesan, I wallowed in anger and regret over what my family had done.

Landing in Halifax, Nova Scotia, I again traveled west on the transcontinental railway, surviving only on wafers and bologna sandwiches while I kept to a strict budget. With such a poor and limited diet, I was fortunate not to break out in another case of hives. Remembering the previous lunch debacle in Calgary, I made sure to steer clear of anything labeled "ham."

By May of 1955, I was back in Vancouver. A friend from work met me at the train station when I arrived and informed me that my old job was still waiting for me. What luck! Soon after, I found myself a nice (yet small) apartment and resumed work with my prior employer.

Because I wanted to further improve my English, I decided to enroll in a local university. I even considered taking a number of other courses on various subjects in the near future, since increasing my knowledge and exploring new possibilities through guided study seemed like an appealing pursuit.

Things were going smoothly, and my life was pleasant overall. In June, a girlfriend from work expressed an interest in going out to a local music and dance club, and encouraged me to join her for the evening. Recalling the fun times at Hammersmith Palais in London, I thought "Sure, why not?"

Figure 56. Passing by Mount Stephen, British Columbia, on the Canadian Pacific Railway.

Partway through the night, as I was enjoying the upbeat music and minding my own business, a young man approached and asked me for a dance. I wasn't particularly interested, but not wanting to be rude, I accepted and said yes. Oddly, we proceeded to dance together for quite awhile without saying one word to each other. He wouldn't even smile or look me in the eye. This young man seemed very awkward and insecure, I thought to myself; but hadn't he been bold enough to ask me for a dance?

He continued to dance with me in aloof silence for the next ten minutes. By this time, I had decided I didn't like him one bit – I thought he was just plain standoffish and unfriendly! I was beginning to bid him goodbye when he finally opened his mouth to speak, introducing himself as Helmut. Right away I noticed his thick German accent. Now this was quite unexpected!

Out of curiosity and surprise, I began to converse with him in our native language. So of course, with me being Austrian and him being German, the ice was broken.

After only a couple brief hours of dancing and shallow chit-chat, Hel somehow convinced me to date him. He was extremely persistent about it, and not wishing to be rude, I obliged him. None of our meet-ups were very exciting, as I had no spending money and neither did he. After a few dates, he began to show up unannounced at my apartment on a frequent basis. We developed a rather ridiculous routine wherein he would start to knock on the door of my little apartment about half an hour after I got home from work. He was always hungry and expected me to cook for him!

The first time he invited me over to his so-called "apartment," he finally revealed that he was living very frugally in a single rented room. The place was always dark, and unusually Spartan and empty; one could see nothing but newspaper spread all over the floor. His only possessions, other than the clothes on his back, were an old pair of blue jeans and a frying pan. These types of surroundings were alien and a bit scary to me, as no matter where I went, I always found decent living quarters and established myself comfortably within a short period of time. He, on the other hand, was struggling even to scrape by and survive.

As far as his personality was concerned, I found him dull, and quite frankly, pesty and annoying. I was not particularly interested in pursuing this dating routine with him. I found the whole thing boring and tiresome. When Hel noticed that I was beginning to express disinterest and push him away, he devised a new plan.

On Wednesday nights, I used to do my laundry downstairs in the basement. I had a comfy little upstairs apartment which included a cooking facility and a sizable closet, but I had to leave in order to use the laundry room downstairs. Somehow, my crafty suitor figured out my weekly routine - no doubt by keeping a close watch on me at all times - and started to bring me his laundry each Wednesday night, so that I could wash it for him. I thought this was very strange.

Not long after, he began to bring me flowers. But these weren't ordinary bouquets; these were colorful garden flowers planted in decorative ceramic pots. I couldn't help but wonder from where he got these. When I pressed him regarding the origin of the flower pots, he stammered for awhile, but eventually admitted he stole them from other people's porches! My jaw dropped in disbelief.

To Hell and Back

Now I was really fed up with him. I told him straight out that I wasn't interested in pursuing this relationship any further, and so we broke it off.

Or so I thought...

Figure 57. Totem poles in Stanley Park, Vancouver, British Columbia.

Maria Rosa

My Stalker

I felt truly relieved to not have to see this thieving and burdensome man anymore. No more dates, no more laundry, and certainly no more dinners – yes!! Peace at last!

Ten days went by, during which time I didn't see him, believing this relationship to be finished once and for all. In fact, it wasn't actually a relationship, it was merely an *acquaintanceship*; there was no intimacy involved, and I didn't even feel an emotional connection with him. Hel was certainly not the caring and affectionate type; I didn't even consider him to be a real man - In my perspective, he was more like an immature and selfish little boy who pretended, and outwardly failed, to be a "man."

One Saturday afternoon, after saving a little money, I went into a beauty parlor to have my hair done. While the hairdresser went to work, I sat in my chair, calmly oblivious to anything out of the ordinary. After the hairdresser was finished, all of a sudden I got a shock: I glanced up and saw Mr. Wrong dawdling into the salon! Perplexed, I could not understand how he knew, after ten days, that I was in the beauty parlor just now.

In retrospect, I am sure he had been stalking me all this time and carefully observing what I was doing, even though I didn't see him in the act. And somehow, naïve fool that I was, he convinced me on the way out of the salon to start dating him again. Of course, I subsequently experienced the same problems all over again with him too – including him knocking on my apartment door and asking for food shortly after I got home from work.

Food and money were already scarce for me, even without his demands; I had only one stove burner, so there was usually no choice but to cook something up in one pot. For me, it was "One Pot Sunday" every day, by necessity. Given these circumstances, I thought it was very unusual that he would beg his way into my apartment for food all the time, rather than asking me out to eat once in awhile – which he never did.

When we dated, we never went out for dinner, never went to a movie, never did anything wherein there would be any money involved. Instead, he would drive us around Vancouver in his friend's old jalopy - to sit by the river, sit by the ocean, or even just sit in the borrowed car. Perhaps he thought this was "romantic." One thing was for sure: he liked to sit. I was usually bored out of my wits. In fact, he was the most boring man I had ever met!

During our many hours of dull conversation, he gradually painted a blurry picture of his personal history. He was from Berlin, Germany, raised as a foster child in a boy's camp in Czechoslovakia, and claimed to have been brought over to Canada by the Lutheran Church in 1952. Whenever I would ask any questions or press him for details regarding his background or past, he would suddenly grow very quiet. What was he hiding, I wondered?

Shortly after, he awkwardly proposed to me. I wasn't expecting this at all. And I was so torn – for about two weeks, I wrestled day and night with the question, What should I do? Should I marry him? Should I, or shouldn't I??

Thrice Enslaved

Never before had I seriously considered tying myself down with marriage and a family. I cherished my freedom; I still wanted to travel, to learn, and to explore. Even though Mario and I had been in love, we never pressured each other to make a solemn commitment, nor even discussed the possibility. A marriage proposal was such a foreign concept to me that I had no idea how I should react.

Wallowing in uncertainty and discomfort, I figured it best to delay my decision. I told my suitor I needed time to think about it. But this answer didn't satisfy him: the more vague and indecisive I grew, the more persistent he became. Soon, Hel begged me daily to marry him. What an oddly obsessed fellow, I thought!

He was truly dedicated to achieving his goal, and in some way this impressed me. I began to try to rationalize the situation in my mind; I thought about my hard-working father and the many wealthy businessmen he associated with, believing that my wooer, being German, would also turn out to be an industrious, goal-oriented, conscientious businessman as he grew older and more mature.

Since my suitor refused to take no for an answer, I eventually agreed to marry him. He then insisted we tie the knot as soon as possible. Being very inexperienced with men or relationships, I wasn't aware of the usual formalities involved in becoming engaged, such as the waiting period which normally ensues before marriage, allowing both parties to adequately plan for the event and be certain they have made the right decision.

Before the wedding, he expressed the desire to live in a furnished room, requesting to move into my little private apartment. I refused, feeling this would be ridiculous and overly cramped for both of us. Instead, I found another apartment suitable for the two of us, and with money I had recently received from my father as a gift, I bought us a bed, a dresser, and a couch. We moved in the night before our marriage - only two weeks after we had become engaged.

The following morning, the weather was dreary as could be, and rain was pouring down. He insisted we follow through despite the darkly ominous storm, so in mid-September, 1955, we got married in a plain civil ceremony at a public courthouse in Vancouver. There were no witnesses present except for the one official who read us our vows.

As I stood there awkwardly in the courtroom with my over-zealous bridegroom, my mind raced. Suddenly I was faced with the gravity of my decision. Realizing I had not yet told my parents about any of this, I quietly panicked. What would they think? How would they react? Am I making a horrible mistake?

In my severe hesitation, I stood stiff and silent as a board, unable to say yes. After a brief pause, the official repeated my vows and asked me again if I wanted to marry this man. Lost in worry and indecision, again I couldn't answer. My fiancé fiddled nervously and looked at me with a blank stare. The official must have realized my hesitation and uncertainty, as he repeated the question a third time, enunciating the words more slowly and with even more emphasis, as if to make sure this was really what I wanted.

Stuck between a rock and a hard place, I softly answered, "Yes."

As soon as our vows were completed, my now husband acted as if, to his great relief, he was a mighty conqueror who finally declared himself victorious over his greatest challenge. It was as if a mask had been peeled off his face, revealing the seemingly friendly Dr. Jekyll to be, in actuality, the cruel and evil Mr. Hyde.

It was still raining, and we hadn't eaten any breakfast that morning. We had been up all night, moving into our new apartment. Rather than taking us out to a nice restaurant, he insisted we have lunch at a local café. We sat on barstools at the coffee counter, where he ordered us the 95 cent lunch special. Our wedding meal was a cheap sandwich plate, washed down with water. I felt depressed and degraded, and already started to have regrets.

That night, rather than enjoying a honeymoon dinner or any sort of festivities, he brought out a loaf of old bread and fixed us salami sandwiches in our newly furnished apartment. I didn't like his salami at all, so I ended up munching on dry bread while he sat there like usual, talking and smoking a cigarette. When he was done, he demanded sex, before callously turning over and snoring.

My wedding day was the most miserable and humiliating day of my life.

Figure 58. Vancouver, British Columbia, Canada, in the 1950s.

Something Smells Fishy

I knew I shouldn't have said yes. But I was, admittedly, a foolish young lady, only 23 years old and very inexperienced with men. My husband could sense this and immediately took advantage of my vulnerability. Now that he had finally gotten what he wanted, his congenial façade melted away and ceased to exist.

I received no gifts from my husband, and certainly no honeymoon. Our modest wedding rings were purchased with money from my father. Within a matter of weeks, both of our rings disappeared. I soon came to realize that Hel had become a very heavy smoker, and such a repulsive and oppressive habit must have cost dearly even then.

In my young adult life, I had never much minded when people smoked on occasion; I took no special notice of it. In fact, early in our courtship, I had even offered my suitor a cigarette or two. What a senseless mistake that was! My spouse now took this as a green light to puff away day and night, without any regard for my health or preferences. I greatly resented him for this never-ending cloud of stink, and soon learned to despise smoking. To this day, I cannot tolerate anyone smoking near me.

A couple of months into our marriage, my husband brought home a bag full of dozens of smelts he had caught – very small fish that are similar to sardines. In Canada, it is common to batter these fish with flour and spices, fry them, and eat them whole. But before walking out the door with a grunt, he immediately demanded that I gut these tiny creatures one by one and cut off their heads and tails before cooking them. Incensed at his rudeness, and already exhausted from a full day of work, I sighed with exasperation and decided to ignore his unreasonable demand.

Frying the fish would have been my first choice, but we were still without any proper cookware. So I opted for the only alternative I had: throwing the smelts into my large crock pot and cooking up a tasty fish stew. A couple of hours later my husband returned, expecting to fill his belly for dinner.

As Hel walked through the door, he whined and groaned about the fishy smell produced by the simmering stew. Addressing me like his personal slave, he screamed at me for "disobeying" him and blamed me for "doing it wrong."

At my wit's end, I told him that next time he wanted me to prepare tiny fish, he could do it himself - or even better, eat nothing!

Figure 59. A heap of smelts.

Penny Crimes

My high hopes for an industrious husband were completely dashed. On a daily basis, Hel demonstrated himself to be lazy, selfish, domineering, and overly critical. Never did he express any love or affection towards me. He refused to hug me or cuddle with me and declined any opportunity to enjoy quality time together.

Hel was only concerned with his own selfish interests. He would frequently demand sex, even when I was feeling unwell. When I told him I was exhausted and would appreciate if we would simply spend some quiet time together, he barked, "What else is there?" Indeed, his self-centered lusts and vices would endlessly consume him for decades to come.

At our dining table, my husband was particularly fond of German-style boiled potatoes, and refused to eat his potatoes served any other way. These were prepared first by peeling, and then boiling them in salt water. Hel began to complain about "my wastefulness" when I peeled the potatoes; he then tutored me, with an authoritarian tone, how to use the paring knife to peel as thin a layer as possible, in order to leave the maximum amount of potato intact. Whenever I lacked the time and patience to peel them with utmost care and precision, he would accuse me over the dinner table of being unthrifty and wasteful.

At the grocery store, Hel would argue with me every time we shopped, demanding that we buy only the lowest-priced items – except when it involved his personal preference for German bread, salami, and smelly aged cheese that stank like sweaty old socks.

Due to the diversion of resources for the war effort, and the ensuing food shortages during World War II, butter had been internationally rationed until 1955, and was still expensive – quite out of reach for us at this point. As a popular alternative, margarine produced from hydrogenated vegetable oils was frequently advertised on commercial television, and various companies were vying with each other to produce a margarine that tasted similar to butter. Prior to 1955, artificial coloring was legally prohibited from being added to the stark white product, so margarine was often sold with packets or capsules of artificial yellow dye, which consumers had to mix by hand. But now, these prohibitions had been removed and margarine could be sold in colored bars, with an appearance pleasantly similar to butter.

I was anxious to try this new and improved margarine, especially a certain popular brand which was known to produce sticks with both the taste and appearance of butter. But my husband refused, arguing that we should only buy the OTHER margarine that cost one penny less per package. ONE CENT! The cheaper margarine was hard, white, and quite frankly did not taste very good. I was embarrassed even to have such a ludicrous discussion in front of everyone in the store.

By now, one could guess that my husband was not truly concerned with economy or savings. Indeed, Hel didn't have our best interests in mind as a married couple; he was only concerned with keeping a constant supply of cigarettes to feed his growing addiction. I began to feel helpless about our finances. To make matters worse, Hel was equally fond of his beer, and demanded that we always have a case of beer on hand, in the event he wanted to idle on the couch in his boxer shorts and drink the night away.

As for the margarine, these "partially hydrogenated vegetable oils" contain harmful artificial trans fats, which the United States is now in the process of banning due to health concerns. The FDA no longer recognizes them as "safe" and asserts that thousands of heart attacks and deaths could be prevented each year simply by taking them off the market.

Figure 60. Vintage margarine ad, with yellow dye mixing bag.

ABC
Chained to Wedlock

After six months of devastating marital enslavement, I was severely regretting my decision to marry this man. I had not yet become pregnant, and was considering options for pulling away from this degrading relationship. But as soon as Hel noticed that I was beginning to grow more detached and distant, he launched an all-out campaign to get me pregnant. And he succeeded.

So here I was, stuck in an abusive marriage with a baby on the way. Divorce at this time was still a dirty word, and having a child out of wedlock, even worse. My parents would have been furious. So I resigned myself to my fate, hoping for the best but still expecting the worst.

My husband showed no concern, and took no effort to help us prepare for the baby. Nor did he care one bit about reducing my stress or workload during pregnancy. He continued to puff away on his cigarettes, and never hesitated to blow the smoke into my face, regardless of the health hazards for both myself and the child. Most of the money Hel earned from his low-wage job was squandered on his smokes and beer, so I had no choice but to continue working full-time at my own job in the bookkeeping department throughout most of my pregnancy.

To make matters worse, our current apartment manager did not permit babies on the premises, and was already pressuring us to move out. Hence, about a month before my due date, we went in search of another place to live. Our only viable option turned out to be a small, dark, and dreary one-bedroom basement apartment. I worried that such cramped and poorly-ventilated quarters would not be healthy for the baby, but what choice did we have?

Then one day, after moving into the basement apartment before attempting to make further plans for the big event, I got an unfortunate surprise: my water broke – two weeks early.

Figure 61. Lion's Gate Bridge, Vancouver.

A Labor of Love

When my water broke, I immediately alerted my husband. I was anxious to get to the hospital, but we currently had no car. He was terrified and could not fathom what to do. Rather than taking any constructive action, Hel planted himself in front of the kitchen sink, and in a panicked fury, proceeded to wash his hands compulsively for the next hour. He was unresponsive to my calls for help, and I wondered if he had lost his mind.

Desperate, I was finally able to contact one of our neighbors who did have a car, and she graciously drove us immediately to a nearby Catholic hospital which was recommended to me by a co-worker.

Labor was intensely difficult, and I was overcome by waves of agonizing pain. The Catholic Sisters in their black and white nun's habits surrounded me in a flurry of concerned activity. A nurse proceeded to administer a shot and told me to "go to the bathroom." I managed to take only a few steps toward the direction of the ladies room before I blacked out.

When I woke up the next day, I was apparently heavily sedated, because I felt like I couldn't move. I was greeted by one of the Sisters, who informed me that my Chinese doctor had successfully delivered my healthy (although small and underweight) newborn daughter, but I remembered absolutely nothing of the labor and delivery. The Sisters told me I had been in such distress that I literally bit one of the nurses on the arm. They giggled and brushed it off, but I failed to see any humor in the situation.

I was also informed that I experienced medical complications, although the nuns never told me what actually transpired while I was unconscious. As a result, they kept me and my newborn in the hospital for ten days, during which time I didn't see hide nor hair of my husband. When I inquired about Hel, they informed me that he hadn't been in the hospital, awaiting my recovery. In fact, he hadn't even seen his baby daughter yet: rather, he had dashed out the door like a crazed chicken after I entered the maternity ward!

Some years later, I learned from a friend that during those ten days, my husband had been spotted around town with another woman – his mistress.

On Hands and Knees

Thus, near the end of 1956, my daughter Jeanette was born, with much hardship and strife. After waking up, I spent another ten days in the hospital, gathering my strength. Hel was still nowhere to be seen.

.After a number of persistent phone calls, the hospital was finally able to get hold of my wayward husband. When he walked in and saw his daughter, instead of being joyous or proud, he had only one thing to say: "Oh. I was hoping it was a boy."

I was so infuriated I could have punched his lights out. But my better judgment told me to remain polite and swallow my anger and humiliation for the sake of the child. I asked him, "Have you bought any diapers?" "No." "Have you bought any formula?" "No, I didn't buy anything. I didn't want to spend the money."

Now, since my daughter was born two weeks early, I was not prepared with the usual necessities. After I was discharged from the hospital, I told my husband to drive us to the apothecary (pharmacy) in his borrowed car so we could pick up some supplies. He knew I still had difficulties walking and would need further time to recover, but when I asked him to go into the store and buy these items, he refused to get out of the car. I begged him, but no – being seen with diapers and formula in public was just too feminine for his macho sensibilities.

Exasperated and exhausted, I took the bull by the horns and got out of the car myself, leaving him to sit there with Jeanette in the parking lot until I returned. I was so weak that I fell to my hands and knees twice before even reaching the entrance door.

Looking back toward the car, I could see my husband was either oblivious or completely without sympathy. Shopping was torture, and my whole body was aching by the time I returned.

We could not afford a crib, nor was there room for one in our tiny basement apartment, so with my remaining money I bought a baby buggy, which for the time being had to double as a crib. My husband made no effort to curb his smoking in front of the baby, nor to even step outside once in awhile to spare her from exposure to the noxious fumes. Enraged at his revolting inconsideration, whenever Hel would puff his smoke in the direction of Jeanette's sweet and delicate face, I tried to shelter her within a small closet that was relatively empty of clothes.

Figure 62. Modern Vancouver skyline.

Maria Rosa

Motherly Instincts

For about a year, I continued to suffer from severe pain and other symptoms caused by medical complications while giving birth. I was unable to work due to the incessant discomfort, so in order to pay the bills I went on disability and collected benefits. Fortunately, the Canadian government also sent me a $500 bonus check for being a mother, as at that time they were promoting family expansion through monetary incentives. Meanwhile, my husband continued to work here and there on part-time minimum wage jobs, but I never saw any of that money.

I was too weak to breastfeed without help, and my body was producing too little milk as it was. We were still without a refrigerator, so I was dependent solely on powdered formula and water to feed my baby. My doctor had given me detailed instructions on how much to feed her and how often, and how to measure out the formula. I followed his instructions as carefully as I could, but something just didn't seem right; Jeanette was always hungry and hardly seemed to grow at all. She was crying a lot and wet her diaper every hour or two. Between feeding her and changing her diapers, as well as washing the cloth diapers by hand in the bathtub, I could hardly get any sleep.

Exhausted and fed up, I decided to try it my own way: I began to feed her more often, and with a higher proportion of powdered formula, until I sensed that she was actually satisfied. And it worked – Jeanette finally began to put on some weight and sleep for longer periods of time, without wetting herself constantly. I noted to myself that a mother's instinct was just as important as a doctor's advice.

After about three months, I observed that Jeanette was growing too big for her baby buggy. I told my husband, "We really need to get her into a crib so she can move and sleep comfortably. Let's look for another apartment." He agreed, and this time he settled on a one-bedroom attic apartment in a less desirable part of town. It certainly wasn't much of an improvement, but it did have a small extra room on the side that was big enough for Jeanette's new crib.

Sometime after we moved in, I noticed my husband had stopped wearing his wedding ring. Startled, I asked him what happened to it. Hel replied, "Oh, the gasman stole it." But we had no gas meter, and I found out later that he had pawned it for cash – the same ring that I bought him with my own father's money! In fact he was happy to be without it, as he didn't want to advertise to other women that he was married.

Our neighbors downstairs were two young ladies who never seemed to sleep, and frequently hosted loud parties with several equally-noisy guests. Sudden bursts of laughter and ear-piercing screams would accompany blaring radio music heard from below, along with the sounds of shattering glass from broken wine and beer bottles. This commotion always upset Jeanette, and I would spend many hours trying to console her.

To make matters worse, my husband's smoking, drinking, and obnoxious friends always took priority over his little family. One night, he brought a group of his own buddies into our apartment and proceeded to play cards on our dining table. As the hours slipped by, Hel gambled, gossiped, and puffed away furiously, completely oblivious to the stress this was causing for both his daughter and me. I was exhausted, Jeanette was colicky, and I could not get her to stop crying. All I wanted was some peace and quiet.

At around 1 am, I was in the kitchen washing the dishes from our previous meal, when my husband walked in and demanded that I make sandwiches for the group. I could feel a migraine headache coming on. In sheer exasperation I screamed at him, telling him that I was exhausted, my head was pounding, we were out of money, and now he expected us to give away the last of our food by serving sandwiches to strangers? He raised his hand to slap me, and in that moment I remembered the humiliating slaps I so unjustly received from my mother. Enraged, I smacked him square across the face before he could touch me, and warned him to never, EVER try that again.

My husband raced out of the kitchen like a chicken and started telling his buddies what had happened. They apparently found this episode very entertaining, and did their best to mock and make fun of me. As they settled down for another round of cards, Jeanette raised her voice and screamed even louder. I was surely at my wit's end.

Devastated, I phoned my doctor, explaining in tears what had happened. I told him the baby was sick and I just couldn't do it anymore. With great compassion, he drove out to the apartment at 3 am, took care of the child, and commanded the gambling party to leave immediately lest he call the police. I was ever so grateful.

When Jeanette was about eight months old, I had recuperated enough to go grocery shopping once in awhile. I returned one afternoon to the attic apartment to find my husband in bed with an "ex-girlfriend" from Edmonton. She had just moved out to Vancouver, and when she called him up he was quick to encourage a "meet and greet" while I was gone with Jeanette. He had not yet informed his "ex" that he was now married. Disgusted, I chased them both out of the bedroom and told the woman that she was never welcome here again.

Over the following few months, I saw my husband only rarely. Most of his time was spent elsewhere – with his mistresses behind my back. Although deeply hurt and angry, I was glad to have the time alone, and devoted myself to nurturing Jeanette as best I could. I grew ever more certain that I wanted a divorce, but I was far too apprehensive to proceed – would Hel take my daughter away from me?

Figure 63. Hotel Vancouver, opened in 1939.

Maria Rosa

Dislocation

I returned to work one year after Jeanette was born. My former boss was again happy to see me, and immediately reassigned me to my old cost accounting position. Shortly thereafter, he gave me training for an advanced accounting job in the financial department. I enjoyed my work and everyone in the office was good to me, but by today's standards the wages I received were very minimal - not enough to adequately support a family. As such, these times in Canada were extremely frugal for us. However, I delighted in being able to buy a fresh strawberry shortcake at my neighborhood bakery for only 75 cents!

My commute to and from work necessitated a long and tiresome bus ride which kept me away from home for longer than I was inclined. I asked my husband if we could find an apartment in a nicer part of town, closer to my employment, for the sake of our daughter, and he was surprisingly agreeable. This allowed me to spend more time with Jeanette, and less time commuting on the bus.

Despite this advantage, as a young wife and mother I was leading a very stressful, poverty-stricken life. My husband's earnings were a pittance, while he continued to smoke and drink heavily. Working was not his idea of time well spent, and he despised anything that required promptness, organization, or discipline. He even refused to wear a watch!

By contrast, I worked overtime to ensure our survival as my baby was growing up; day and night I occupied my mind with complex and tedious tasks as a "bean-counter" in the import firm's financial department, just so we could afford our apartment and have a little food. I had nothing extra to spend for my baby, so when she needed shoes, I had to purchase them at a second-hand store. This turned out to be a terrible mistake, as she developed problems with her feet due to the ill-fitting cheap shoes. Later on, her gait had to be corrected with orthopedic shoes.

I continued to endure much disappointment and heartbreak from my husband. Each time I bought him a holiday present with my father's money, it never failed to disappear – even a bathrobe was nowhere to be seen. Loyalty was a foreign concept to him, and he was a terrible liar as well. He did not wish to behave like a married man, or even be a father to his child. At times I felt so desperate that I only wanted to run away, even if I had to seek the charity of strangers. But I decided, once again, not to rock the boat.

The constant grief and stress gradually built up within me and found its only outlet in a severe outbreak of acne on my face. I had to go on sulfur treatments and antibiotics for my skin.

My health suffered in other ways as well. Not being able to afford proper winter clothes for myself meant countless hours of shivering in the cold rain while waiting for the bus, and this too took its toll: I suffered one cold after the next, which my husband's smoking only exacerbated.

Things turned from bad to worse as time went on. One evening, I came home from work to find Hel in our front room with a French-Canadian woman I had never seen before. They both appeared disheveled. He had cooked dinner for her and left me a mountain of dirty dishes. The kitchen was in such a shambles that I was unable even to find the teapot so that I could make myself a hot cup of tea, much less cook anything for myself.

Walking out of the veritable disaster zone, I heard Jeanette wailing and rushed to her aid. To my horror, her shoulder had been partly dislocated from its socket. My husband had apparently yanked her arm and pulled too hard. I immediately called the doctor and he instructed me on how to gently manipulate her shoulder to snap it back into its socket. He later confirmed that she was very fortunate not to have suffered any long-term injury.

As my husband grew more reckless and distant, I had no other choice but to hire a babysitter who could provide daycare for Jeanette while I was at work. One of my co-workers recommended a friend who could supervise the baby at her house for a reasonable cost, any day of the week. One evening after work when I went to retrieve Jeanette from the babysitter, I walked in to find her standing precariously at the top of the stairs, crying with her panties pulled down around her ankles. I was in shock and despair to be confronted with such a sight. I immediately grabbed my child and told the babysitter we would not be returning.

In late 1959, when my daughter was three years old, my husband was fired from his job after attempting to unionize a shop with three employees. His boss evidently considered Hel to be a threat to him and his business, and proceeded to spread this news to similar shops throughout the city. Nobody wanted to hire Hel after that.

With my husband's prospects for employment in Vancouver virtually destroyed, it appeared that we would no longer have a future there. My mind raced, searching for a solution.

California Dreaming

When I informed my father about our dire straits, he exclaimed, "Come back home to Austria! Bring your daughter and your husband with you. I'll hire him, and he can work in the family business for good pay." I readily agreed to my father's life-saving generosity

Hel and I proceeded to sell off the furniture and household goods we had accumulated over the last four years. I already had our tickets in hand for the *Saturnia* and the transcontinental rail to New York City. My father sent us $5000 cash to help us with our travel and accommodation costs, which I allowed Hel to manage.

At the last minute, when we were all set to go and board the train, my husband suddenly changed his mind: "I don't want to leave," he said. Shocked, I replied frantically, "This is ridiculous. We're all set. We have to leave now." "No. I just don't want to go," he said, offering no explanation.

Infuriated, I pressed the issue. "What the heck are we supposed to do then? Are we just supposed to throw our tickets into the rubbish bin and live on the streets?"

"We'll move into a furnished room," he replied.

I must admit I strongly entertained the thought of boarding the train with my daughter and leaving him right there. But my father would have been greatly dismayed by such an act on my part, so I felt I had no choice but to cooperate with my husband's irrational wishes. I found us a small but decent furnished room, with a pull-out bed nestled into the wall.

After about three weeks in these cramped quarters, I pressed the issue again. "We can't stay here. It's no good for Jeanette, and everyone in your field of employment is blackballing you. Without you working, we can't even pay for daycare. Let's move out of this city so you can find a job."

Silence. He acted completely disinterested in what I was saying.

"Please. Think about it. ...Do you remember that TV show you liked so much, the one filmed in San Diego, California? That looked like a nice place, didn't it?"

"Yeah."

"Then let's go to San Diego and see if we can make a better life for ourselves." To my surprise, Hel agreed, and said he would take care of obtaining our immigration visas.

For months I waited patiently for any news, but nothing came. Growing more suspicious by the day, I ventured a look into the drawer that used to hold the visa applications, and discovered that my husband hadn't even submitted the paperwork yet. My heart sunk in despair.

To Hell and Back

Part Four: American Dreams

Figure 64. American flag.

Maria Rosa

The Roadtrip from Hell

Taking the bull by the horns, I submitted the visa applications myself. Since we were already Canadian citizens by that point, our U.S. immigration visas were granted by spring of 1960.

After my positive experience with the Freemasons in Manhattan, had I been on my own I would most likely have opted to return to New York. But now, with a family to care for, I felt that would be impossible. So instead, my husband and I made preparations for the long road trip to southern California. To scrounge up as much extra money as I could, I sold off any extra baby clothes and toys which we didn't need anymore.

I was still entrusting Hel with the $5,000 from my father. At every turn, when it came to our preparations he stalled for time and moved at a snail's pace. Later on, I heard from a friend that my husband admitted he was contemplating returning to Germany with all the money, while leaving Jeanette and me to fend for ourselves.

Since he still didn't own a car, I gave him $500 to purchase a nice used vehicle. Strangely, he settled on a flashy pink Ford. I always wondered why he chose such an unusual car - one seemingly very out of character for him; later he revealed that he was planning to quickly re-sell it for cash in California.

Initially, the scenery during our trip was beautiful; as we drove south, we passed through Eureka and the great redwood forests of northern California. Despite the spectacular landscapes, this road trip was one of the most terrible and miserable journeys I have ever undertaken.

My husband refused to stop driving under any circumstances – not for lunch, not for dinner, not for a bed to sleep in, and not even for a toilet break at the rest stop unless he deemed it convenient for himself. As we drove through the forests, he provoked many arguments and screamed like a maniac. We found out later that Hel was thinking of dumping Jeanette and me in the wilderness so that he could take off with the money and continue driving to California alone.

Needless to say, our four-year-old daughter was growing quite cranky; she was tired and hungry, but this didn't make any difference to him. He demonstrated absolutely no compassion or empathy for either one of us. For a whole week, we lived on practically nothing but dry old bread and sausage, and tough salami which the child couldn't even eat.

Yes, it took us almost a whole week to arrive in San Diego, even though we drove along the Pacific coast. These routes were still unfamiliar to us, so I suspect we took quite a few unnecessary detours. He also refused to let me drive the car he had purchased.

Finally we arrived in San Diego, hungry, miserable, and exhausted. However, this city was not what we were expecting to see from the television shows; the weather was chilly and windy at this time of year, and poverty appeared prevalent. It seemed as though we had been under an illusion created by clever scripts and carefully edited camera-work.

Instead of finding a hotel room so we could clean ourselves up, eat a decent meal, and get rested, he insisted on driving right away through a dirty-looking, impoverished neighborhood with the intention of finding another cheap room to rent.

I was extremely dissatisfied with this scenario and grew unhappier by the minute. Thinking of Jeanette's future, I refused to settle for the same situation we had left behind only a week ago, and demanded we turn around and head back to Los Angeles.

Figure 65. Foggy redwood forest in Northern California.

Deserted in Hollywood

We arrived in Los Angeles the following day, still hungry and unwashed. Again, rather than finding us a hotel room so we could relax and wash up, immediately my husband began hunting for a cheap apartment in the North Hollywood area. He settled on a shabby and rather squalid furnished flat, and promptly asked me to supply the money for the rent deposit.

Perturbed, I told Hel to take the funds out of the $5,000 cash from my father that he was still carrying around. Upon hearing this, my husband glanced downward and nervously shuffled his feet. Clearing his throat, he told me that the money got "lost" when he "transferred it to New York." The entire sum had supposedly just disappeared into thin air, and he offered me no explanation as to why he even sent it to New York in the first place. Were it not for the last $500 in my wallet, which I was keeping as an emergency reserve, we wouldn't even have been able to pay for a roof over our heads!

During our married years in Canada, we had always depended on the monetary gifts we received from my father. But I never saw a penny of the $5,000 I entrusted to him, and now we were left with practically no money at all.

Later on, I found out that Hel had sent the money to another woman back in Germany - perhaps an ex-wife or a first wife. Back when I first met my husband, he had shown me a photograph of a four-year-old girl, whom he claimed was his niece. However, since Hel was in fact a foster child, he never had a niece, and the little girl looked exactly like my daughter did when she was about four years old. The similarities were striking. To this very day, I suspect he left behind another family in Germany before latching onto me in Vancouver. He would continue to send money to Germany for decades to come.

We settled down in that dilapidated flat, located in a crime-ridden neighborhood where I felt very uncomfortable, and absolutely miserable. What was going to become of me and my daughter? I worried.

As Jeanette was now only four and a half, I needed to find daycare located within a reasonable distance. Trying to make the best of a bad situation, I asked my husband if I could borrow the pink Ford so I could take her to daycare and find work as soon as possible, since I had no idea how our next month's rent was going to be paid. That same week, the car disappeared as well.

My husband claimed the Ford was smashed up in an unfortunate auto accident. Although we had Canadian insurance, I never saw a penny of it, nor even an accident report. Later on, I found out that he had sold the car for cash to pay for his heavy smoking and drinking.

Hel soon lapsed again into all of his old habits, spending much of his time away from home. Disheartened, I felt virtually abandoned there in North Hollywood with my child.

Emergency Calls

After much urgent prompting, my husband finally found a job with a refrigeration company in downtown Los Angeles. His duties included cleaning out old refrigerators for $80 a week. Within an hour's walking distance of our flat was a friendly Jewish deli, where I also obtained a 9-to-5 job. Next door was a private nursery school, so at the end of the day my daughter and I walked home together, hand-in-hand.

Often, Hel would claim that his work hours were extended on so-called "emergency calls"; as such, there were many evenings when he didn't come home until midnight. His absences were usually unpredictable and he provided little information, so I often sat there late at night in our cheap apartment wondering if he was ever coming back again. These same excuses continued for the entire year of 1961. Later on, I found out he was visiting his various mistresses during these extra "work" hours.

By the time Jeanette turned 5, I had accumulated some savings from my job and insisted that we move into a better neighborhood. My husband decided on a dilapidated old house in Panorama City which we could move into with no down payment. He occupied himself with renovating the pathetic fixer-upper, but wouldn't allow me to express my opinions or make any decisions regarding the renovation – not even to buy curtains for the windows. And he still came and went as he pleased.

As my daughter was now old enough for kindergarten, he demanded that I enroll her in a Lutheran school, since he was raised in a Lutheran boys' camp. Since I was raised Catholic, I hadn't the foggiest notion about Lutheranism, but I obliged him nevertheless. Many of the teachers and supervisors seemed friendly enough, until Jeanette's birthday came around.

I brought a large birthday cake to the private school, expecting the children to celebrate together and for my daughter to partake of a slice, just like any other birthday. But at the end of the day, I was informed that the kids weren't served any cake at all. (Did the office staff take it home and eat it themselves?) Instead, Jeanette had received a cheap hot dog which promptly gave her food poisoning. All night, she was suffering from nausea and stomach pains. Infuriated, I pulled her out of class immediately and enrolled her in public school.

By early summer of 1962, Jeanette had finished her first year of public school. At this point, I decided I was not willing to endure any further grief from my cruel, arrogant, cheating husband. Instead, I was planning to return to Austria with my daughter and leave him for good. Packing up my few suitcases with the intention of never coming back, I told Hel that I was going to visit my family with Jeanette, and departed LAX on a Pan American flight with a pair of tickets from my father.

An Unwelcome Visitor

Upon our arrival, my parents came to pick us up at the Vienna airport. My father was so pleased and excited to see me with my little girl that he ran and leapt with joy as soon as we appeared – he was beside himself with delight! My mother, on the other hand, expressed no emotion at all, and really appeared quite sour. This hurt and confused me, but I decided not to say anything in front of Dad.

The good times didn't last very long. After about two weeks, my mother and brother started to act funny towards me, while my father seemed to suffer from bouts of sadness and grief. Evidently, I was a thorn in my brother's eyes, and an unwanted inconvenience to my mother. I slowly began to understand why they resented my presence so much: As my father was a well-to-do businessman who had accumulated a sizable estate, he was expected to pass along all of his wealth to his first-born son – my brother Frank; whereas, a daughter like myself simply did not fit into this old-fashioned picture of life. I was supposed to be married off to another wealthy businessman, make myself disappear, and never be a "burden" on my family again.

But here I was, a reminder of all they had never wished to be held accountable for. On top of that, they still considered divorce to be a dirty word, and did not like the fact that I had separated myself from my husband. Regardless of the emotional torment I endured throughout my marriage, my mother would often say, "You better go back to him."

On the other hand, Father wanted me back in business with him, and even offered to buy me a house; but I could hear my mother arguing with him for days in the back room. Finally, after I had been home for 3 weeks, she walked up to me with a grimace on her face and proclaimed, "I will never look after your children."

My jaw dropped in shock at my mother's sheer animosity and lack of compassion. After hearing this proclamation from her, even if I were to resume working in my father's business, I felt that Jeanette would not be safe with my family, as it was now clear they regretted my very existence.

By now, my husband noticed that I had packed all of my personal things into my suitcases, leaving behind only what belonged to him. Panic apparently set in, and I received an unexpected phone call from him. Hel asked me when I was coming back, and with a soft, sweet-as-honey voice that belied his forked tongue, told me "Oh, *things are going to change, I promise.* Things are going to get better now. I'm gonna do this, and I'm gonna do that, and I'll make sure to be a good husband and a good father. I'm a different man now." Where have I heard that one before, I thought sarcastically to myself.

Ultimately, this was all just a big lie. I found out from friends later on that he was certainly not bemoaning my absence; rather, Hel had just spent two weeks on vacation in Mexico, drinking, gambling, and having a good time with women on the beach.

I didn't believe his promises, of course; but I found myself in quite a predicament. My mother obviously had no intention of helping me care for my daughter while I was expected to work for a living and attend exhibitions with Dad. Jeanette hardly knew one word of German yet, so going to 1st grade in a school where she didn't understand the language would have been pure misery for her; as a newcomer and an outsider, she probably would have been bullied and harassed by the other children as well.

Jeanette hadn't learned German because my husband hated my Austrian accent and refused to listen to what he called my "hillbilly dialect," while at the same time I despised his unusually harsh and obnoxious Berliner accent. (I couldn't understand half of his words, but I sure didn't speak hillbilly!) As a result, we never spoke German together, especially in front of Jeanette.

But given all of the above, I decided that going back to the United States was probably the best thing I could do. I still loved my father dearly, as he always did his best for me, but after this maltreatment I could never feel the same way about my mother or brother again.

Figure 66. President Kennedy signs the Proclamation for Interdiction of the Delivery of Offensive Weapons to Cuba at the Oval Office on October 23, 1962.

The Cuban Missile Crisis

Shortly after Jeanette and I returned to the United States, the infamous Cuban Missile Crisis commenced in October of 1962. For a seemingly never-ending two weeks, the entire nation was caught up in a frightful uproar, aware that the world was teetering on the brink of a global nuclear catastrophe. Every day I sat on the edge of my seat, waiting apprehensively for any news about how the situation was developing.

The Cold War between the United States and the Soviet Union was in full swing, and the Missile Scare - which also involved Soviet ally Cuba – is regarded historically as the first time the threat of mutual destruction was a determining factor in the making of a major international arms agreement.

After a failed attempt by the U.S. to overthrow Fidel Castro's Cuban regime during the Bay of Pigs Invasion, Soviet Premier Nikita Khrushchev forged a secret agreement with Castro to place Soviet nuclear missiles on Cuban soil to deter any future invasion attempts. The Kennedy administration opted to respond with a naval blockade of Cuba, which they referred to as a "quarantine," and demanded that the Soviet weapons be dismantled and returned to the USSR.

Not surprising, Khrushchev was uncooperative, sending a letter to President John F. Kennedy, announcing that the U.S. blockade constituted "an act of aggression propelling humankind into the abyss of a world nuclear-missile war." Despite the extreme tension, Kennedy and Krushchev began secret negotiations to resolve the crisis. In the meantime, the U.S. and Soviet militaries came within a hair's breadth of global nuclear devastation several times, during a number of nail-biting confrontations.

Finally, on October 28, 1962, Kennedy and the United Nations Secretary-General were able to reach an extensive agreement with Krushchev, thereby ending the crisis. After realizing the dire need for a quick and clear communications line between Washington and Moscow, a direct telephone link between the U.S. President and Russian Premier was also established. Further secret talks ensued with Cuba's Fidel Castro as well.

A friend informed me during this time that instead of the usual fire drills, public schools were now practicing "drop-and-cover" drills to "prepare" the children for imminent nuclear war. There was also a run on the supermarkets, leaving many shelves bare. Between the turmoil going on in my personal life and the international drama on the news, I was growing ever more fearful and upset. What kind of crazy world were we living in, I wondered? What kind of suffering would future generations be forced to endure if so-called "modern civilization" couldn't even refrain from self-annihilation on a massive scale?

Figure 67. President Kennedy and Secretary of Defense Robert McNamara discuss the Cuban Missile Crisis.

The Assassination of JFK

President John F. Kennedy was a favorite of the American people, and after defusing the Cuban Missile Crisis he came to be widely regarded as a national hero. But then, on November 22, 1963, shots were fired that were heard round the nation: the assassination of JFK.

President Kennedy, with First Lady Jacqueline Kennedy Onassis, was publicly making his way through Dallas, Texas in his Presidential motorcade when a hidden sniper fired the fatal shots. An investigation later concluded that he was assassinated by Lee Harvey Oswald, a former U.S. Marine who had defected to the Soviet Union in 1959 and subscribed to Marxist ideology.

This horrible event shocked me, and stunned countless millions of people worldwide. For the next four days I was an emotional wreck, glued to the television set. In the hours following the assassination, the entire nation was reeling, thrown into a state of deep disorientation and confusion. With the recent Cuban Missile Crisis fresh in public memory, the United States was still mired in the frightful distress and uncertainty of the Cold War, and no one knew immediately whether or not the Kennedy assassination was the beginning of a larger attack upon the United States; nor did they know if Vice President Johnson, who was riding only two cars behind in the motorcade, was still safe.

People wept openly in public, gathering together to grieve as they watched the coverage on department store television sets; spontaneous prayer groups formed, entreating God for mercy and protection;

To Hell and Back

Figure 68. President Kennedy just before his assassination.

traffic in some areas ground to a halt as word-of-mouth spread from vehicle to vehicle.

I too was in tears, utterly devastated by the news. Staring at the TV in a daze, I was overwhelmed by the situation and its potential implications. As I tried to pull myself together, I wondered why we had ever left Canada – I had a good job, lots of friends, I was even enrolled in university; my life had been just fine – until I met my husband!

Nor did this national tragedy soften my husband's heart, not at all – he only became meaner. For days he fomented unnecessary fights and arguments between us, knowing it was an emotionally charged time period for me. My daughter was now attending elementary school nearby, within a 15-minute walking distance. I usually picked her up after school, but on one such day he dragged me into another argument and wouldn't let me go; when I realized how late I was, I rushed out the door, only to find Jeanette walking home by herself, crying her heart out and wondering if something bad had happened to me. Her sense of safety and emotional security had also been worn away by the national panic which had been piled on top of the family drama.

Figure 69. President John F. Kennedy and Lyndon B. Johnson in front of the White House.

His *Other* Other Family

In terms of national events, the ten years I had spent in Canada were quite peaceful, socially and politically. I was not used to such upheaval anymore; now, after the Kennedy assassination, I felt like I was suddenly revisiting the distraught wartime turbulence of my childhood. Memories came surging back, along with their associated emotions.

Vice President Lyndon B. Johnson was sworn in as President of the United States within hours of Kennedy's assassination. During his earlier years in the House of Representatives, Johnson had been a close ally and informant of President Franklin D. Roosevelt, and I soon learned that Johnson had also played quite a key and pivotal role in World War II.

After America's entry into the Second World War in 1941 following the Japanese bombing of Pearl Harbor, Johnson became a commissioned officer in the Naval Reserve and, under special assignment by President Roosevelt, reported to General Douglas MacArthur as part of a Southwest Pacific survey team. Soon after, Johnson also reported back to Roosevelt and Congress about the nation's critical need for more war supplies, military cooperation, and experienced men in the Pacific Fleet. Johnson's mission immensely aided the United States' overall war effort and military strategy. But he wasn't without a comical side as well: many recalled, with a smile, stories of a black presidential Lincoln Continental careening down a dusty road through his Texas ranch, with empty beer cans flying out the open window!

Kennedy's assassination deeply affected me emotionally, but as the nation tried to pick itself up and keep moving forward, so did I. My husband, however, suddenly decided that we should move our residence. We sold the old renovated house and got just enough money to make a down payment on another small home in a different county. This new town we moved into was just developing; the population count was low, and there was not even a nearby freeway yet. The setting was so suburban that my daughter and I really felt "out in the sticks" compared to what we had grown used to.

After moving house, I barely saw my husband anymore. Throughout the whole of 1964, he was away day and night on his "emergency calls." Whenever Hel did come home, the phone would ring at odd hours - midnight or two o'clock in the morning, for example. He acted extremely hateful toward me and showed no love for Jeanette; in fact, I was almost afraid for her safety when he was around.

When my daughter was about 8 years old, Hel came home one day and abruptly asked me to adopt a certain infant boy, telling me that he still wanted a son. Wondering why he was so adamant about this particular child, I did a little investigating, which led me to another shocker. On many occasions during recent years, he had been smoking and drinking the night away at a bar located near our previous homestead. It came to my knowledge that Hel had had an affair with the bar owner's German wife - and this woman was the mother of the boy he now wished me to adopt.

And the German mother? Well, she was now attempting to hide the fact that she had committed adultery and given birth to another man's son. My husband, not wanting to give up the boy, had agreed to adopt him in order to conceal the affair from the bar owner. I refused however, realizing that Hel had moved us into this dusty, distant town because his illicit affair had been too close to home.

A few years later he showed me a recent picture of the boy, whom he was still fixated on, and the boy looked exactly like my husband did in his own childhood photographs. I could have sworn Hel had fathered a carbon copy of himself!

Figure 70. President Franklin D. Roosevelt shakes hands with a young Lyndon B. Johnson in Texas on May 12, 1937.

Open For Business

By 1968, all three of us were United States citizens. But we still had very little money for ourselves – my husband continued to make only $80 a week, working small jobs. When Hel had started out, he had no trade or formal career training; but over the years he accumulated some industry know-how and work experience. For Jeanette's sake, I desperately wanted to improve our standard of living, so I asked my father for money that would enable us to buy a commercial truck and equipment, in order to start a business of our own.

I was confident we could make a success of it. After all, I was educated in business management back in Europe, and I never had any difficulty finding work; my supervisors often praised my job performance, and my friends told me I was charming and personable. Self-assured, I firmly believed that "where there is a will, there is a way."

When we received the money from my father, we formed a corporation and bought the truck, tools, and equipment Hel needed. I answered the phone, took care of all the secretarial duties and office work, as well as the accounting – yet I wasn't supposed to pay myself one penny for the household expenses. Everything was "his."

With my help and hard work, the company grew profitable and expanded; but as soon as Hel started to accumulate more money for himself, our marriage went from bad to worse. My husband grew even more verbally abusive: At this time, I was still an attractive young lady in my 30s, and polite men were quick to compliment me on how pretty I looked. Whenever Hel became jealous of the attention I received, he lashed out, calling me an "old bag." When I wanted to wear a fashionable peace sign mini dress, he told me I had "ugly legs" – fearful that other, more worthy men would glance at my attractive figure. He was certainly no supermodel himself! His jealousy was so intense that he even did his best to stop me from socializing with male friends.

On the other hand, my father, delighted at the prospect of another successful family business, sent my husband many nice gifts as a gesture of support, such as work boots, professional tools, and even a hunting rifle – but not once did my father ever receive a thank you from Hel. Nor did my husband ever write him, call him, or have any desire to visit him, as my father would have wished. He never expressed any affection or fondness for anyone – and not once did I ever hear "I love you" from him.

Despite all these insults and disappointments, I continued to stay with Hel, as my daughter was still going to school and I didn't have the funds necessary to make any major life changes.

Figure 71. Buzz Aldrin salutes the U.S. flag during the Apollo 11 Moon landing.

Maria Rosa

The Moon Landing

On July 20, 1969, my husband insisted on dragging Jeanette and me to an upscale Korean restaurant so that he could watch the Apollo 11 lunar landing on the eatery's large color television set. It was a momentous and historically significant occasion, being the first spaceflight that landed humans on the Moon, broadcasted on live TV to a world-wide audience.

All 3 of us were seated at a table with a good view of the action. After the waitress served an appetizer of *kim chi* (pickled cabbage), the lunar module landed on the surface of the Moon. Eagerly shoveling the *kim chi* into his mouth, my husband ordered an extra bowl, commenting on the fact that it reminded him of his favorite *sauerkraut* – pickled cabbage prepared in the traditional German way.

Hel stared, enraptured with the scene on the television, while devouring every last morsel on his plate. Several hours went by as the astronauts, including Americans Neil Armstrong and Buzz Aldrin, prepared to exit the craft. Suddenly, Hel got a distressed and surprised look on his face. Pushing back his chair, he ran awkwardly to the restroom.

Six hours after landing, Neil Armstrong became the first man to set foot on the surface of the moon. Armstrong and Aldrin spent about two and a half hours outside the lunar module, collecting over 47 pounds of moon dust and rock to bring back to Earth. The Apollo 11 mission effectively ended the Space Race with the USSR and fulfilled the promise President John F. Kennedy made in his 1961 speech before Congress, in which he proposed a new national goal, "before this decade is out, of landing a man on the Moon and returning him safely to the Earth."

My daughter and I watched in awe as Neil Armstrong stepped onto the lunar surface in his spacesuit and uttered his famous quote: "One small step for man, one giant leap for mankind." My husband during this time, however, was communing with his moon rocks while experiencing his own private moon landing in the restroom. His moon rocks had a splash landing!

Figure 72. Neil Armstrong on the first Moon walk.

Maria Rosa

Freedom from Oppression

Our business was thriving, only because I took care of all the phone calls, advertising, bookkeeping, and many other duties. However, with his pockets now lined with cash, my husband rarely came home anymore. Near the end of 1969, he didn't return for a whole week, and I wondered what was going on.

Then I received a speeding ticket in the mail: Hel had been pulled over by police in Hollywood at 3 o'clock in the morning. Shocked, I decided to do some investigating.

Subsequently, I found out that he had been living full-time with yet another woman, a mother of three children. Enough was more than enough, so I decided it was high time for me to file for divorce.

Before leaving for good, Hel scoured our entire house and emptied the premises of anything he deemed "his." He went so far as to take the kitchen utensils, the coffee table, the flower vases, even ripping out the air conditioning unit which I had paid for with my father's money, so that he could install it in his mistress' stuffy apartment.

In 1970 my divorce was finalized, and I can honestly say that it was the happiest day of my life! I felt like I had been freed from Nazi oppression all over again. That day, I was released from 15 years of misery, 15 years of wasting my young life, and 15 years of painful and demeaning abuse. My daughter still talks to me to this very day about Hel's vicious and ruthless behavior, and the distress he consistently inflicted on us.

Despite his compulsive lying and cheating, during my entire 15 years of marriage I was as loyal and faithful as could be, in every way, shape, and form - to the point of being ridiculously old-fashioned and perhaps even stupid. I often ponder why I ever married Hel, and I come to the conclusion that I didn't actually want to; rather, he pushed and pursued me so hard, in effect actually stalking me, that I took pity on him and felt moved to help him improve his life. He knew he couldn't support himself, and obviously saw a good thing in me - a kind and compassionate young lady who was foolish enough to tolerate him and his vices. I often wish I would have been smart enough to walk away from him as soon as I had sensed that our relationship wasn't right for me.

Figure 73. Collapsed freeway overpass after the 1971 Sylmar earthquake.

Maria Rosa

The Sylmar Earthquake

After the divorce, my father, expressing concern and dismay, sent my brother to California in order to "check up on how we were doing." Frank stayed with us for a week, acting as my father's liaison by inspecting our house, possessions, and overall situation. When my father inquired about his prior "business investments," he was informed that my husband had taken the business, the money, and even the company vehicle for himself, leaving us with almost nothing. Frank also reported that we were "living in a shack" and merely scraping by under "pathetic circumstances," which was certainly a mean-spirited exaggeration, especially after we fed, housed, and entertained him at our own expense for a week.

Father was furious, as well as deeply disappointed. Divorce remained a dirty word back in Austria, and he seemed to regard my present situation as shameful and unbecoming. In years past, he had always sent gifts and much-needed cash, no matter what difficulties or challenges I faced; but as soon as he heard my brother's slanderous report, he demonstrated his displeasure by ceasing to offer any further gifts or help, apparently perceiving his former aid to have only been a business investment which unfortunately had gone down the tube. Much to my chagrin, this meant that when Jeanette and I needed help the most, we didn't get anything from anybody – I didn't even receive alimony.

While I was re-adjusting to life as a single mother, on February 9, 1971 another tragic event struck: the Sylmar Earthquake. This was the first earthquake I had ever experienced, and I found it very strange to feel the earth moving and shaking beneath my feet. It was an altogether alien sensation. Windows and doors rattled eerily as knick-knacks flew off the shelves; other household items tipped over and rolled back and forth.

I was scared of course, but at this time I was living quite some distance from the epicenter, so damage in our neighborhood was minimal. However, in the following days I was deeply affected by what I saw on the other side of the hill. Several major freeway interchanges had collapsed, along with numerous buildings. City streets were faulted and uplifted, and roadways were closed. Hundreds of landslides occurred, and 64 people had been killed.

Following these calamities, suddenly, out of the blue, I received an unwelcome phone call from my ex-husband. His business office was located nearer to the epicenter, and he gave me a short and whiny spiel about the earthquake, whereby he tried to induce me to take pity on him. Then, in one of his typical Dr. Jekyll and Mr. Hyde maneuvers, Hel abruptly assumed a commanding tone of voice and barked, "Those five-gallon water bottles. You still have them. Bring them over to my office this afternoon."

After questioning him further about his situation, it soon became clear that nothing was preventing Hel from obtaining his own water and restocking his own supplies at nearby stores. He was in no immediate danger and suffered no lack of essentials; rather, he was simply using the situation as an opportunity to try to crawl back into my life and abuse my kindness once again. Nor did he even ask if Jeanette and I were safe after surviving the same earthquake.

Fed up with his manipulating tactics, I was certainly not about to let this cold-hearted control freak take over my life once more. Gathering all my inner strength, I voiced a firm NO and told him never to call me or darken my doorstep again.

Hanging up the receiver with a bang, I shut that door for good.

Figure 74. Fragmented freeway, 1971 Sylmar earthquake.

The Longest War

The years following 1970 were extremely difficult for us financially. Meanwhile, the Vietnam War raged on. In 1964, Congress had passed the Gulf of Tonkin Resolution, allowing President Lyndon B. Johnson to dramatically escalate American involvement in the war, in an attempt to prevent the communist takeover of South Vietnam. U.S. casualties soared as the peace process suffered continual setbacks. Massive bombing campaigns were ordered against strategic cities in communist North Vietnam, while millions of gallons of toxic Agent Orange herbicide were sprayed on Vietnamese land. Despite sustained violence and conflict from 1956 onward, the war showed no signs of ending, and the public at large began to seriously doubt the Johnson administration's optimistic claims that a victory was close at hand. Growing unease prompted a large and angry antiwar movement, especially on university campuses, as well as rioting in major cities.

Jeanette graduated early from high school in 1972, at the age of 16, as she was eager to enroll in university. She started attending classes at state university later that year, on a campus fairly close to home. She told me that many of her friends were grieving for older siblings who had been lost or injured in the war, while debates raged on about whether or not America should continue to remain involved in the conflict. No family was left untouched by the ravages of war.

During this time, photojournalism grew in prestige and importance, becoming a vital means of documenting current events as they happened. Jeanette sharply recalls the horror she felt when she first viewed the famous 1972 photograph of a little

Vietnamese girl, Phan Thị Kim Phúc, running naked down a road with her siblings after a napalm bomb was dropped on her village by the Vietnam Air Force. The child had survived only by tearing off her burning clothes.

Matters grew even more grim in 1972-73 as the Watergate Scandal erupted into the public media, revealing a series of clandestine and illegal activities undertaken by members of the Nixon administration. President Nixon, facing imminent impeachment and loss of political support, resigned from office on August 9, 1974, asking the nation to support his successor, President Gerald Ford. In his televised resignation speech, Nixon attempted to defend his record and reputation, quoting from President Theodore Roosevelt's 1910 speech *Citizenship in a Republic*:

"Sometimes I have succeeded and sometimes I have failed, but always I have taken heart from what Theodore Roosevelt once said about the man in the arena, 'whose face is marred by dust and sweat and blood, who strives valiantly, who errs and comes up short again and again because there is not effort without error and shortcoming, but who does actually strive to do the deed, who knows the great enthusiasms, the great devotions, who spends himself in a worthy cause, who at the best knows in the end the triumphs of high achievements and who at the worst, if he fails, at least fails while daring greatly.'"

Eventually, American-allied South Vietnam came to be perceived as doomed, and the Vietnam War largely regarded as vain and hopeless. A cease-fire was brokered following the withdrawal of US combat forces in 1973; however, North Vietnam once again resumed the war in 1975. In response, Congress declined to provide any more funding for further combat operations or resupply missions. On April 23,

1975, President Gerald Ford gave a televised speech declaring the end of the Vietnam War, as well as all U.S. aid. My daughter vividly remembers being in the elevator on her way to her political science class that day, when she heard this news by word-of-mouth. The sense of relief was palpable as the announcement spread throughout the hallways and classrooms of the campus.

However, U.S withdrawal resulted in the capture of Saigon by the communist North Vietnamese Army on April 29, 1975. Martial law was declared, and a frantic evacuation operation proceeded to remove U.S. diplomatic, military, and civilian personnel out of harm's way via helicopter. Fixed in Jeanette's mind are the photographs of the chaos and panic that broke out as South Vietnamese civilians and officials scrambled to escape Saigon. In the early morning hours of April 30, the last U.S. Marines were evacuated from the Embassy by helicopter, while civilians stormed the walls and poured into the embassy grounds - but time had run out. Formerly employed by the Americans, these civilians were now left to their fate at the hands of the North Vietnamese.

The war had exacted a huge cost in terms of human fatalities. Over 58,000 U.S. service members had died in the conflict, while over 150,000 had been wounded in action. Millions of Southeast Asian civilians and service members had also been killed.

The capture of Saigon marked the end of the war, but it was not an end to the atrocities. In the following months, South Vietnam, Laos, and Cambodia were overrun by the Communists. Millions of Southeast Asians were murdered in the years to come, as the Communists consolidated their power and eradicated anyone whom they perceived had previously resisted them or allied themselves with the United States.

Maria Rosa

Whole families and children were not spared. Millions more were imprisoned or forced to flee, resulting in the largest flood of refugees since the end of World War II.

Unfortunately as well, since Vietnam had been a very unpopular war, the veterans who returned home were often received with palpable resentment or even hatred. Some members of the public felt that these veterans bore a share of the blame for what had transpired. Many suffered from irreparable physical and psychological damage. Struggling with post-traumatic stress disorder and unable to find work, some opted to "self-medicate" with addictive drugs, or had already become addicted while in Vietnam.

In 1976, with the recent events still fresh in the nation's memory, Jeanette graduated from university with honors and enrolled in graduate school.

Figure 75. Vietnamese civilians hiding in a water-filled ditch.

Energy Crisis

Due to our financial difficulties, it took ten years, from 1970-1980, for my daughter and I to elevate ourselves to a lifestyle that was even considered normal by American standards. The U.S. economy was suffering, jobs were hard to find, and salaries were generally low. Due to my training in accounting and business management, I was fortunate enough never to have problems finding a job, but my pay was often disappointingly meager.

Between the demands of work and school, Jeanette and I were usually so busy that we weren't able to keep up with local events, or familiarize ourselves with what was happening around us. Often, we didn't even have enough time or money to go grocery shopping, so for a few years we survived mainly on ramen noodles and microwave spinach soufflé.

Needless to say, I was under a great deal of stress. Sleep and relaxation were hard to come by, and I was often downright exhausted. Even so, I was willing to pay the price: as I was an educated woman who had benefitted in myriad ways from my knowledge and independence, I wanted nothing more than for my daughter to enjoy the same. Her father had always looked down on such an idea, saying "there's no law in this world that a girl has to have an education." A dust pan and a frying pan – that was all a girl was entitled to in Hel's eyes. But I would have none of that; instead, I always emphasized the importance of my daughter's well-rounded education.

From 1976 onward, Jeanette attended graduate school in Los Angeles for a professional degree, while living with me at home. As such, transportation was a difficult issue for us, so most of the time we shared a car in order to save on expenses and gasoline. During her last four years of school, we were practically living on the freeway – coming home at midnight and leaving again at five o'clock in the morning, while she studied in the car as I drove. I would then drop her off and proceed to drive to work. At the end of the day, I picked up Jeanette from graduate school and commuted back home. Wash, rinse, repeat, in a seemingly never-ending routine.

To make matters even more stressful, in the wake of the Iranian Revolution came the 1979 oil crisis. Iranian oil exports were suspended, and oil prices shot up amidst widespread panic and fear. After a partial reactor meltdown at the Three-Mile Island nuclear power plant, national anxiety further increased with regard to energy policy and availability. Long lines appeared at gas stations, while fuel was rationed in many states. Due to our personal situation, I was able to obtain a special permit to tank up as often as necessary; however, costs were sky high and we often had to idle in slow-moving lines at the gas station for two hours or more, while wasting precious fuel. Before this time, car model designs had grown larger and larger, guzzling ever more gasoline as fuel efficiency decreased; but now, manufacturers were beginning to successfully release more compact, fuel economy vehicles.

Unable to afford most routine car maintenance, let alone a new vehicle, one rainy morning the brakes on our overused car gave out amidst start-and-stop rush hour traffic on the freeway. The only way I could bring the vehicle to a stop was to turn off the ignition and wait for the car to lose momentum. Add to this the fact that our gas tank was running low as I repeatedly had to start and kill the ignition whenever the traffic changed. While I felt that I had relatively good control over the vehicle and its speed even though our tank would soon run empty, Jeanette was terrified and regarded it as the scariest ride of her life. This incident caused her to feel even more determined to achieve professional success and financial independence.

In order to save on gasoline costs, I began looking for work closer to the graduate school. Through a CPA firm, I was able to locate a job with an Iranian Jewish family in Beverly Hills who had fled to the United States during the Iranian Revolution. My workplace was based inside a large skyscraper overlooking the city. I occupied myself daily with accounting and office management, while outside the windows, far below, I could see Gucci handbags being offloaded from trucks in the courtyard of another building.

My boss would often fondly mention a friend of his, named "Bijan." Eventually I found out that this person was Bijan Pakzad, the famous Iranian designer of fashion menswear and fragrances. In 1976, he established an exclusive boutique on Rodeo Drive in Beverly Hills. Some have called the boutique "the most expensive store in the world." Out of sheer curiosity, I wanted to take a look inside and maybe even say hello to Bijan; but when I visited one day, the doorman told me that no one could even enter the premises unless they already had made an appointment in advance.

Bijan went on to dress some of the world's most influential men, including Presidents Barack Obama, Ronald Reagan, and George W. Bush, as well as Arnold Schwarzenegger and Tom Cruise, amongst many other famous faces.

Meanwhile, news grew even more tense. After a group of Iranian students took over the U.S. Embassy in Tehran, 52 Americans were taken hostage. They were held captive by the ringleaders from November 4,

1979 to January 20, 1981, while the students attempted to extort the United States with numerous political demands in support of the Iranian Revolution. President Jimmy Carter emphasized that the "United States will not yield to blackmail," but his approval rating plunged as he failed to bring a satisfactory end to the crisis.

However, on January 20, 1981, at the very moment when President Ronald Reagan completed his inaugural address after being sworn in, the 52 hostages were released into U.S. custody after spending 444 days in captivity - thus setting a remarkable tone for the start of Reagan's presidency. Hope was restored, and a new page had been turned in the history of the nation.

Figure 76. Lines at gas station during the Energy Crisis, 1979.

To Hell and Back

Part Five: Global Connections

Figure 77. Sydney Tower, Sydney, Australia.

Life and Death

By the end of 1980, my daughter had finished graduate school and obtained her professional certifications. I was not doing so well, however: the constant stress and exhaustion had taken their toll, and gradually I grew more and more ill. Without divulging the gruesome details, one day I was bleeding so heavily that I was rushed into emergency surgery.

I remained in recovery in the hospital for a whole month. Meanwhile, my daughter felt virtually abandoned, as she was without any help or support, emotionally, financially or otherwise. In need, she reached out to a bright young man whom she trusted as a friend, and as time passed, their relationship grew and deepened. After recuperating from my surgery, I was eventually able to return to work, although I was still weak.

My granddaughter Alexis was born near the end of 1981, six weeks early. As she was a preemie, she had to stay in the incubator at the hospital for more than a month. Jeanette and I were both working full-time, so every night after work we drove together to the hospital to see the baby. She was the cutest little thing you could possibly imagine! Even if I grow to be a hundred years old, I'll never forget the day Alexis turned around and looked right at me with her big blue eyes, wide open with curiosity!

I was, however, greatly displeased with the hospital staff. A lot of the nurses were quite abusive, showing little regard for the health and welfare of the babies under their care. They did not hesitate to play music at high volume, make loud noises next to the incubators, and forcefully rip the nipples out of the babies' mouths when bottle-feeding.

Alexis developed bradycardia, a slow heartbeat, which is common when preemies temporarily stop breathing due to their immature development. After a month of nightly observation, we were finally able to bring her home, weighing barely 5 lbs. The hospital bill amounted to over $10,000, which was a very large sum back then. They insisted that we pay every penny, even though Jeanette had no health insurance. Absolutely no one would help us - not even my own father, who was still disgruntled with the idea of my divorce.

After bringing Alexis home, a new professional career position awaited my daughter, so she went back to work while I looked after the baby. While Jeanette slept at night, I stayed next to the little one, who was on a heart monitor for the next three months. After six months, we were finally able to pay off the hospital bills.

In 1982, when Alexis was 9 months old, I got news from Austria that my now 73-year-old father was very ill. Worried, I purchased airline tickets with Lufthansa for myself, Jeanette, and Alexis. Our subsequent travel preparations turned out to be extremely strenuous and expensive. My parents' old house was not properly equipped to lodge a baby, and my mother warned me that any supplies, even formula, would be hard to come by in the local stores. So we packed about ten suitcases and carry-on bags to take along with us, which included everything from a stroller, to a baby bed, to formula and bottled food, diapers, wiping cloths, and anything else we needed for the baby. I felt like I was about to embark on a year's journey!

Maria Rosa

All in all, after departure it took approximately 18 hours to arrive in Vienna, Austria, which included a switch of planes in Frankfurt, Germany. After landing and fetching our 10 suitcases, we met up with my brother, who was supposed to pick us up from the airport and drive us to my father's house. Since Frank "didn't want to damage his new car with our luggage," he brought his old jalopy and stuffed the baggage into the back.

Such a trip by car should have taken two hours at most on the freeway. However, for some reason my brother decided to use only offbeat surface roads and made frequent stops. On one particularly desolate back road near the Hungarian border, he insisted on stopping around 5 o'clock in the afternoon to slowly eat a mottled, rotten-looking apple which he pulled out of the trunk. In the meantime, it was getting dark. I couldn't understand why he was unnecessarily prolonging what was already an exhausting journey. Finally he got moving again, but strangely, he then pulled over a few more times along the route. When I questioned him, he only offered lame excuses.

As a result of my brother's hesitation and delays, the drive took us 8 hours instead of 2, and we arrived home in the dark at 10 pm. We were all exhausted and hungry, and the baby was crying miserably. Later on I found out that Frank was debating in his mind whether or not to dump us at the Soviet-occupied Hungarian border, where we'd be at the mercy of whoever found us on the edge of Communist territory.

Once home, my brother shushed us, telling us to be quiet because Dad was ill. For our living quarters, we were given the dusty old attic room that I had as a child. From the moment I entered the house, cold shivers came over me again, just like during the war.

For one reason or the other, this particular house always left a bad taste in my mouth – too many painful memories from my youth.

I asked Frank to help me take the bed and formula upstairs for the baby so that we could warm up some milk and put her to sleep, but he said "No, leave it. We'll do that in the morning." I begged and asked him what was I supposed to do with a crying baby then? He finally relented, grumbling under his breath and acting like the favor was a tremendous burden for him.

I finally saw my father the next morning. When I greeted him, I got the shock of my life. He was a man that I did not recognize. I had only been told that my father was sick, not that he was deathly ill. I hadn't realized until now that he was actually dying.

Betrayal

I hadn't seen my father in 20 years, but I never expected him to look like this. He was emaciated, had lost all of his teeth, and couldn't walk without leaning heavily on a cane to support himself. He was also in a great deal of pain and discomfort, and drugged so heavily with pain medications that he seemed out of his mind. The drugs made him extremely cantankerous, very unlike his old self. My mother, who was only 69, was so worn out that she looked like 90.

Every time I tried to go into my father's room in order to speak with him alone, Frank made an immovable obstacle out of himself, telling me not to disturb him. Father eventually emerged on his own and came into the kitchen a couple of times, sitting down to read a newspaper; yet instead of talking about anything current or relevant to the circumstances, he rambled on about buying another house in the future. It was impossible to reason with him in his morphine-induced haze. I asked him if he wanted to hold the baby, but he refused, apparently afraid that he was so weak he would drop her.

The beautiful resort town of sparkling rivers, wild berries, and green meadows that I fondly remembered from my childhood was no more to be seen. Everything here now seemed perfectly strange to me. Many of the original buildings were gone, and few people did I recognize anymore. My old homestead, which had always been vibrant and full of activity related to my father's ventures, was now glum, decrepit, and utterly depressing.

Already after three days, the entire situation grew intolerable. My mother had been fairly amicable on the first day of our stay, even presenting us with a small gold necklace as a gift for the baby; but by the second or third day she began to act distant, avoiding any conversation with us. Frank whispered into her ear behind our backs, surely with nothing nice to say.

My parents' antiquated house was dilapidated and downright hazardous, as well as exceedingly inconvenient. The beds in our old attic room were 70 years old, and dreadfully uncomfortable. As soon as it grew dark at 8pm, everyone crept off to bed and refused to have any further interaction.

The staircase was likewise aged, narrow, and creepy, as well as a hazard to navigate. Yet there was no choice but to do so frequently, as there were no bathrooms upstairs - unless one was fond of using Victorian-style chamber pots. The only bathing facility downstairs was a rusted out old tub, which we avoided by cleansing ourselves with baby wipes for the next ten days.

Mother didn't cook for us, as she was usually holed up in the upstairs room watching over Dad, and hardly able to move herself. There was little food in the house, so most of my time was spent grocery shopping, preparing meals in the kitchen, and taking care of baby Alexis. When I brought home a cauliflower, my father demanded it for himself.

My brother, ever eccentric, opened up jars of baby food and sampled them with a spoon, even devouring one for a snack. He went so far as to search through our garbage – too bad he didn't find the dirty diapers!

Jeanette couldn't communicate very well with Frank, but that didn't stop him from bugging her on a daily basis. Whenever she went into the bathroom to do her hair or brush her teeth, he was standing right there behind her, watching her every move with a creepy stare. This greatly irritated her, and she told him in no uncertain terms that he needed to leave and stay far away. From then on, the tension between them was so thick one could slice it with a knife.

To escape this noxious atmosphere, we went on many walks in order to get out of the house as much as possible. We visited my cousin and her family, explored the local historical buildings and churches, and enjoyed the green open spaces that were still left. Jeanette strapped baby Alexis to the front of her body with a rucksack and strolled under the linden trees beside an old abandoned castle.

Nevertheless, the looming and complex family issues continued to weigh heavily on my mind. No one explained to me why my father was in such terrible condition. I suspected that the outlook was not good. Hoping to learn the truth, I began searching through my father's office to see if I could find some medical reports or any further information about his condition. Of course, Frank saw me doing this; immediately, he ran to my father and told him I was "looking for a will" or other legal papers to "see how much money I would inherit." He even claimed that the only purpose for my visit was "to see what I could get."

Now, this was the worst thing anybody could have possibly done to me in that moment. Matters of inheritance were the furthest thing from my mind; if anything, I wished for my father to live to a ripe old age. How viciously my brother twisted everything!

Father was furious, and his demeanor grew even nastier after he heard Frank's slanderous diatribe. To make matters worse, my mother's idea of the rightful order of things was always that my brother would inherit everything. In fact, while I was growing up, she would tell me, "Why don't you leave! You don't have anything here!" Nor was she ever inclined to help or express affection to me, like she would with my brother. Instead, I was always blamed for Frank's misdeeds, with painful spankings and blows as my reward.

Father hid himself away for the next three days. Finally, he re-emerged and asked how much the trip had cost Jeanette and me, so that he could reimburse our expenses, which we needed desperately. I calculated the total amount, and as he placed the cash in my hands, he told me that this was my inheritance, and not a penny more.

Then he hatefully raised his cane at me with a mean grimace. Shaking it and growling under his breath, he said that "he will never forgive me for abandoning my family." I walked out, cash in hand, attempting to hold back my tears.

Father only lived another 3 months.

Insult to Injury

To set the record straight, I did not abandon my family; rather, I was simply desperate to escape my limited and war-torn surroundings so that I could see the world and make something of myself as an educated and independent lady. I had no intention of allowing myself to be stuck in some dark, dusty corner with Mr. Sewermeister and molded according to someone else's concept of what a woman's role in society "should" be. I only wanted to be my own person, but my father, good intentions aside, always found this difficult to accept, much less embrace.

When I was young, restless, and full of dreams, the situation at home with my mother and brother was just as intolerable as it was now, if not worse. My father was usually gone for his business trips, and whenever I spent time with him at exhibitions or in the office, he was always interested primarily in promoting his business. He frequently pushed his older business friends on me, expecting me to agree to marry one of them; I resented this, as I had no interest whatsoever in pursuing a relationship with them. These older men were strangers to me, and far from my idea of a complementary partnership. I was much more inclined to travel, see the world, and create a life for myself that did not conflict with my distinct internal compass.

After my father raised his cane at me, I did not attempt to have any further contact with him. Before leaving my parents' house, I asked my brother to give me a younger and more flattering photograph of my father, as a keepsake to remember him by. To add insult to injury, Frank refused to let it go until I handed him a $20 bill. He then drove us back to

Vienna, where we were scheduled to depart on our flight the next day.

Jeanette and I had already reserved a hotel room, but we had been without food or drink that day, so we planned to find a nice Viennese restaurant as soon as we had checked in. Afterward, I planned to take her to St. Stephen's Cathedral and other places I fondly remembered visiting with Aunt Anna during my growing years.

Without even asking for permission, my brother barged into the hotel room with us and immediately invaded the bathroom. He then took a long, hot shower and flopped himself down on the bed. Jeanette and I couldn't leave, or even clean ourselves up, for fear that he would search through our luggage in the meantime.

Regardless, we hadn't eaten in 16 hours, and our formula supply for Alexis had run out. She was getting cranky, so we had to do something. I invited my brother to eat out with us, and he agreed. We walked around for a while without any luck, as many of the better restaurants had already locked their doors. Finally we settled on the only restaurant that was open at that hour – it looked like a greasy spoon to me, but we were all ravenous anyhow. We ordered some soup, which was supposed to have been "chicken stock," and I fed a couple spoonfuls of clear broth to the baby.

My brother stuck around for another two hours, insisting on browsing through the Viennese shops with us, probably expecting us to buy him a costly parting gift. He kept walking around with his fly open, and when I told him to zip up, he refused and said he was hot. Everyone looked at Frank as if he were crazy.

Yes, yes he was.

He finally left at the last minute, and Jeanette and I rushed back to our hotel room to clean ourselves up, as we hadn't taken a proper bath in ten days. Much to our dismay, the hotel was economizing their heating costs by producing hot water only during certain hours, and my brother had already used up most of the remaining hot water when he took his long shower.

We boarded our plane from Vienna to Los Angeles, but within a short time Alexis started to get ill from the so-called "chicken broth." She was obviously suffering from stomach cramps. During the entire flight I walked back and forth, back and forth through the aisle with her, rocking the baby and trying my best to soothe her, but she just would not stop crying. I was ready to collapse, while other passengers shot us the evil eye and made nasty remarks because they were irritated. No one offered to help, of course.

When we landed, I was so relieved and overjoyed to be back home in the United States that I never wanted to return to Austria again, for as long as I lived.

Figure 78. Peacock at Koala Park Sanctuary.

Aussie Adventures

Jeanette continued to work for a professional firm in Los Angeles until 1985, when she opened her own office in our hometown. We saved every penny we could in order to buy office equipment and furniture, as well as pay for rent, telephone, advertising, insurance, and everything else it takes to run a business. Money was still scarce at first, as we had a lot of expenses; but Jeanette worked very hard, and over the years she began to develop a substantial clientele due to her excellent reputation.

I helped Jeanette with her office while taking care of my granddaughter Alexis, who began attending public elementary school. We started her with private music lessons to learn the piano, with which she demonstrated talent even at a young age. I enjoyed listening to her practicing on the keyboard for hours, and encouraged her to keep up the good work.

Near the end of 1987, when Alexis was about 7 years old, I received a holiday card from one of my old school buddies, inviting me to come to Canberra, Australia for a family Christmas celebration. Erik and I had attended all of the same schools together during our youth, and we each knew the other's family on a personal basis. Erik's father had owned a local chicken farm, equipped with a watermill for grinding flour. Whenever I visited, he would send me home with a basket of fresh eggs. Sadly however, Erik's mother died when she was only 39, and his father was prone to bouts of rage, during which he would mercilessly beat the boy with his heavy leather belt. Erik therefore left that household behind as soon as possible, eventually establishing himself as a construction contractor in Australia, becoming a wealthy businessman after years of hard labor.

I gladly accepted Erik's invitation, and booked a trip to Australia with Jeanette and Alexis for the Christmas holiday. During that time, it was unusually cold in Southern California; in fact, I remember our plants were frozen overnight, and a layer of frost had accumulated on the ground. "Oz" however, being located in the Southern Hemisphere, experiences reversed seasons and thus enjoys Christmas over the summer holidays. What a contrast!

The flight to "the Land Down Under" was long, yet pleasant. After our stopover in Tahiti to refuel, the Aussie flight crew switched to "party mode" and wrapped themselves up in colorful tinsel. One of the male attendants even hung a sparkly tinsel "kangaroo tail" from the back of his pants as he pranced around in good cheer!

We arrived in Sydney on Sunday, in the state of New South Wales, and booked a hotel until it would be time to see Erik in Canberra, located to the south in Australian Capital Territory. The atmosphere throughout Sydney was lightweight and festive; the weather was warm, and many people had been out all night drinking at the pubs. Some were now standing outside, laughing and smiling with bottles of beer still in hand.

In the meantime, Jeanette, Alexis, and I boarded a relaxing harbor cruise, which took us by the famous Opera House while we enjoyed a nice lunch on the boat. Unfortunately, at the time we could not afford to actually attend one of the lavish performances. The next day we did some more sightseeing around the city, browsing through the shops and dining in the Sydney Tower, a landmark skyscraper similar to

Seattle's Space Needle. It is Sydney's largest free-standing structure and features an observation deck with a spectacular 360-degree view of the city.

On our last day in Sydney, we took a two-hour bus ride to Koala Park Sanctuary, a privately owned wildlife park with a famous collection of koala "bears" (although they aren't truly bears, as we were taught). Little Alexis was delighted to learn about the adorable koalas and watch them slowly munch on big bunches of eucalyptus leaves; we also explored the many zoo-style cage exhibits, which included dingoes, cockatoos, kangaroos, and wombats, among other unique Australian fauna. She was particularly awed by the gorgeous peacocks proudly displaying their splendid feather fantails – even though they aren't native to Australia!

After walking around the koala park all day, we were happy to return to Sydney, where we boarded a flight to Canberra on Wednesday.

Figure 79. Adorable koala at Koala Park Sanctuary.

Maria Rosa

A Square Meal

Erik, my Austrian school buddy, eagerly joined us in Canberra (Australia's capital city) to pick us up from the airport. Erik and I hadn't seen each other in 40 years, since we were 18, so it had been quite a long time indeed. Nevertheless, we recognized each other immediately, as if no time had passed. As we reminisced, our familiar, playful dialogues brought back nostalgic memories of our old hometown, as though nothing had changed since the days of our youth!

But some things definitely had changed. Erik was quite the wealthy entrepreneur now, with a beautiful home, numerous business associates, and two grown children, a daughter and a son. He asked us to stay with his family over the Christmas holidays, and supplied each of us with a comfortable, spacious guest room.

With excitement and pride, Erik boasted that his wife Rosella now worked as a professional chef and would be cooking a special turkey dinner at the Christmas gathering he was soon to host for family and friends. In preparation, he laid out a stunning table with seating for 12 while Rosella and her Thai assistant Malai worked together in the kitchen.

Jeanette, Alexis, and I sat down and engaged in animated chit-chat with the other guests while we waited. It was a hot, sunny day – how strange and unusual it was for us to celebrate Christmas in the summer! This really took some getting used to, as the cozy holiday atmosphere we normally enjoyed was just not apparent without the typical wintry weather of the season.

To Hell and Back

Figure 80. Australian magpie.

While roasting the turkey, Rosella briefly stepped out to serve an appetizer. We were presented with small bowls of thin cucumber soup. Sampling the sparse, one-inch-high broth at the bottom of the dish, I quickly arrived at the opinion that it was watery and tasteless, as if our chef had opened a can of instant soup and thinned it out with two extra cups of water. Observing the numerous sour faces around the table, I could see that many others were likewise displeased, but were keeping quiet for the sake of politeness. Alexis hated cucumber soup to begin with, so she didn't even touch her bowl.

As soon as the turkey came out of the oven, I knew dinner would be a disaster. The skin was pale and unappetizing - definitely not like my usual roasted Thanksgiving turkey. When they sliced into the breast, the meat was clearly undercooked, as some parts were still half-raw. Oh my, two older women in the kitchen and neither of them seemed to know what they were doing!

Erik understandably panicked a little at this point and ordered them with a sharp voice to shove the bird back into the oven for a bit. He was so embarrassed that his face turned beet red!

When they finally served the turkey, the ladies cut the meat into squares. Yes, squares rather than slices! Who the heck would serve cubed turkey for Christmas dinner? I began to seriously wonder where Rosella had attended chef school. To make matters worse, the turkey was tough, with some guests barely managing to choke it down as their faces grew more grim by the minute. Alexis couldn't chew hers, so she started crying and left the table hungry. When Jeanette saw this, tears streamed down her face and she excused herself as well.

After dinner, Rosella's assistant Malai visited our

Figure 81. St. Christopher's Cathedral, Canberra.

guest quarters and sheepishly apologized for the lousy turkey, informing us that it obviously wasn't their specialty: "It was Erik's idea." She then invited us for dinner at her house, where she would skillfully prepare "some delicious Thai cuisine" in the traditional manner.

Over the following days, we attempted to relax at Erik's house, located in an exclusive neighborhood frequented by diplomats and foreign officials. Despite the upscale surroundings, Erik could not prevent his home from being invaded by flies. Yet, as annoying as they were, he refused to kill even one, acting as if it were taboo. Rather, he insisted on catching them alive and carrying them outside in a cup, only to have them sneak back in again later.

Alexis was bored and discontented, so when I wasn't out on walks with her, she was usually sitting in the backyard, feeding the neighborhood flock of magpies with pails of raw shrimp and barbecue scraps. She obviously enjoyed her pastime of tossing little pieces of food, one at a time, and watching in fascination as the big black and white birds swooped down to retrieve their catch. I was quite certain the magpies' dinner was superior to what we had received at Christmas!

Erik also showed us some local landmarks, including what is now the Old Parliament House, where Australia's Senate and House of Representatives convened. With its white façade, classical-style architecture, and parliamentary gardens on each side, it reminded me of the White House in Washington, D.C. Alexis was delighted by the bright red and blue Crimson Rosella parrots, also known as the Red Lowry, chattering away noisily in the trees. I smiled to myself and wondered if we might encounter another "crimson Rosella" in Erik's kitchen that evening.

Additionally, our guided tour took us to the beautiful St. Christopher's Cathedral, adjacent to the shopping district. With its striking Spanish Romanesque architecture, St. Christopher's has often been the location chosen by members of Parliament for the year's opening prayers. Canberra and Sydney, despite their unique aspects, reminded me of cities I had seen while living in England, such as Gloucester, due to their many magnificent old buildings with eye-catching Gothic, Victorian, or red brick facades.

We decided to accept Malai's dinner invitation, as her husband Max was a close friend of Erik's, working as a maintenance man on his construction crew. I soon discovered that Max was a crude and hilarious old Austrian hillbilly, originally from a small rural community not far from my hometown. He seemed like a very strange match for his slender Asian wife, but they apparently got along quite well. Perhaps it was her cooking: she prepared a scrumptious Thai seafood and vegetable curry with seasoned fried rice. Everything was delicious indeed, with just one problem: the portions were very small.

And no wonder: to the side of the stove sat a large bowl with a mound of leftover rice. Oddly, Max and Malia did not venture to grab seconds, nor did they ask us if we would like another helping. Not wishing to come across as impolite, we kept quiet. Alexis, however, hadn't eaten much that day and needed more food, so she politely asked if she could have some extra rice. Malia gave her the evil eye and shook her head saying, "No, that was enough." Apparently the two of them were planning to eat the leftovers all by themselves!

Hungry and upset, Alexis started bawling and ran out of the room. So much for a nice family dinner!

Hoping to bring home some healthy snacks for Alexis, I visited an open-air fruit market. The selection was mind-boggling – everything from locally-grown favorites to exotic tropical oddities – but the prices were much higher than I was used to in America, and I found myself unable to afford much on our scanty budget. Before leaving, I made a quick stop at the restroom, only to find myself screaming in horror as two large, hairy black tarantula-like spiders crawled along the top edge of the stall. Eeeeeewwwwwww!!!!!!

I couldn't run fast enough. I'm not sure whether or not they were deadly - but given Australia's infamous reputation for an abundant variety of extremely venomous creepy-crawlies, including spiders and snakes, I don't really want to know!

Maria Rosa

Bushwalk

Following our Canberra tour, Erik informed us that he also had a summer vacation home to the south in Merimbula, where he would like to host us before our departure. We gratefully accepted his invitation, but first he encouraged us all to visit the Tidbinbilla Nature Reserve, which was only a short drive from Canberra.

The reserve is named after Tidbinbilla Mountain, which overlooks a large valley. The name derives from an Aboriginal word meaning "a place where boys become men," as Tidbinbilla Mountain was formerly used as an Aboriginal initiation site.

As Erik pulled into the valley entrance of the reserve, he rolled the side windows down a couple of inches and sat back in his driver's seat, waiting patiently with a mischievous grin on his face. Uh oh, I thought – bratty little Erik is up to no good again! Soon, we were approached by a flock of emus slowly making their way down the asphalt driveway.

As they drew closer, they lowered their necks and swung their fuzzy heads back and forth with curiosity. Considering us with one orange eyeball, and then the other, they seemed to develop a ruthless and predatory glint in their eyes. Their three-toed, taloned feet resembled those of a nimble two-legged dinosaur ready to strike.

Suddenly, these giant, 6-foot-tall ostrich-like birds lunged toward us from all sides, poking their long, sharp beaks through the open spaces at the top of the windows. I screamed in terror, afraid they would poke someone's eyes out! A couple of the emus ominously opened and closed their beaked mouths,

Figure 82. Emu.

as if expecting a handout (or a hand, as the case may be).

Erik just sat there, laughing hilariously at our reactions. He obviously had this all planned out, that skunk! And he surely took his sweet time rolling up the windows! This devilish prank must have been payback for all those times I smacked him as a boy when he was being a bratty and immature little pest.

As if that weren't enough, Erik insisted we take one of the bushwalks through the native habitat. As we walked, Alexis delighted in feeding the wallabies and

Figure 83. Kangaroos at Tidbinbilla.

kangaroos, who nibbled tamely from her hand while standing amidst tall tufts of dry grass. She was lucky enough not to get hurt, and thoroughly enjoyed her little "outback adventure"; I, however, did not fare so well. Forgetting to watch my step, I stumbled upon a colony of aggressive red bull ants, which inflict an extremely painful bite, similar to that of fire ants. All of a sudden they were crawling over my leg, and by the time I could remove them they left me with searing pain and fiery welts. Jeanette too, despite wearing boots, pantyhose, and full-length pants, emerged from the hiking path covered with inflamed welts, as if some nasty variety of stinging critters had crept up her legs to find a meal.

The whole bushwalk experience was frightening to me, and I was so grateful we didn't encounter any snakes or tarantulas to top it off! Erik, on the other hand, just had another good laugh, probably thinking to himself "if you're so dumb, it serves you right!"

To Hell and Back

After a couple days of recovery in Canberra, Erik drove us to Merimbula. Along the journey south, we encountered many beautiful stretches of rainforest. The state of New South Wales is home to over 1200 acres of rainforest, containing many rare and endangered species of plants and animals. Unfortunately, these areas are under threat from mining, tourism, and other industry, and have been steadily disappearing ever since European settlement began.

Erik, ever the impulsive road hog, navigated the highway's many twists and turns at high speed, and the erratic motion was starting to make Alexis feel ill. I told Erik to slow down because she was getting carsick, but he shook his head with a smirk and wouldn't have it. A few minutes later, Alexis projectile vomited all over the interior of his shiny new car. That'll teach Erik a lesson, I thought!

After a good deal of stomach-turning cleanup, we arrived at Merimbula, a tourist town located on the

Figure 84. Merimbula, Australia.

Merimbula Lake near the southern border of New South Wales. Erik's vacation home was situated very near to the ocean - and even in this quaint little town, kangaroos and parrots seemed to be everywhere!

We spent several days in Merimbula. My daughter got along very well with Erik, and enjoyed walking the pristine white sand beaches. The water was so clear and blue that one could view the rocks beneath, and there were no beach barriers to stop people from sauntering right up to the ocean from their front yards and wading in with their bare feet. Alexis occupied herself with looking for seashells and smooth water-polished pebbles.

We also took a ride on a glass bottom boat, equipped with a flat clear glass plane through which we could view colorful schools of fish and other marine life below. Apparently whales and dolphins also frequented the area, but we did not see any that day. Piles of oyster shells had been heaped along the waterway, as Merimbula is renowned for its fresh rock oysters and is home to a substantial oyster farming industry. We finally disembarked on another stretch of pristine white sand beach.

I discovered that there were many Germans and Austrians living in Merimbula, apparently so-called "sea changers" who tired of city life and wished to embrace a more serene and easygoing existence near the ocean. Not all of them however had abandoned their entrepreneurial flair: I happened to come across a traditional German bakery selling delicious but expensive pastry treats. With my limited cash, I settled instead on a souvenir koala figurine cleverly made out of seashells.

Jeanette enjoyed spending a quiet evening outside, lounging in Erik's peaceful oceanside backyard.

Unfortunately, she forgot to cover up, and the next morning she awoke with her legs covered in itchy, sore, red lumps the size of cranberries. She had once again become unexpected prey for Australia's ever-present stealth bomber mosquitoes.

Duty soon called, and in short time we flew back to Sydney. The return flight from Sydney to Los Angeles was extremely stressful. To begin with, our scheduled departure was delayed on and off for several hours as we nervously awaited news regarding a problem with the plane's landing gear. We were finally allowed to board once the aircraft was declared safe for takeoff, but I was sitting on pins and needles during the entire flight, as the plane rattled like a rickety old crate. This jet was the noisiest, shakiest contraption I had ever flown on, and I swore to myself that I would never fly again!

Notwithstanding, we eventually made it back to Los Angeles in one piece. Even though I appreciated my Aussie adventure, it was truly nice to be home again.

Figure 85. Emu.

Maria Rosa

Mozart's Birthplace

As a piano student, Alexis was very fond of classical music, especially the works of Wolfgang Amadeus Mozart. She was interested in learning more about his life and the history behind his music, as well as in having a chance to meet her now 80-year-old great-grandmother. So in 1992, when Alexis was 11 years old, Jeanette and I decided to visit Austria one last time with my grand-daughter.

We boarded our Lufthansa flight as usual, and after an early morning landing, we took a taxi immediately to my mother's house. Alexis was happy to meet her, eagerly offering hugs and kisses, but my mother was as dreary and detached as ever, which somewhat disappointed the little girl. My childhood home was again dark, cold, and unfriendly, and there was little food in the refrigerator, so my mother encouraged us to go out and eat at a nice restaurant for lunch.

It was a perfect opportunity to introduce Alexis to the Wiener Schnitzel, Austria's famous national dish. I must emphasize that a genuine Wiener Schnitzel has nothing in common with Wienerschitzel hot dogs from the popular American fast food chain. A true Wiener Schnitzel is made from thin slices of veal tenderized with a meat hammer, lightly seasoned, and rolled in flour, whipped eggs, and bread crumbs. It is then fried in lard or clarified butter until golden yellow. Pork is also used nowadays, at half the cost. The recipe dates back to the early 1800s, and the dish is traditionally served with *Kopfsalat* (lettuce tossed with a sweetened vinaigrette dressing), potato salad, cucumber salad, or parsley potatoes. It is also common now to serve it with rice, french fries, or

Figure 86. Wiener Schnitzel.

roasted potatoes, and topped with a slice of lemon and a sprout of parsley.

As there were no accommodations for us to stay at my mother's house, I opted to spend the afternoon with her and then proceed to Salzburg, the famous "city of Mozart," with Alexis and Jeanette. With its scenic Alpine backdrop, Salzburg's *Altstadt* ("Old Town") is internationally renowned for its spectacular and well-preserved baroque architecture, and has been listed as a UNESCO World Heritage Site since 1997. Salzburg means "Salt Mountain" or "Salt Castle," deriving its name from the barges which carried salt from a nearby mine down the Salzach River, which flows through the city. These vessels were subject to a customary toll charge, collected by officials in the 8th century AD, ensuring over the following centuries that Salzburg would become a powerful trading community. By 1077, the city's medieval castle fortress, known as the *Festung*

Hohensalzburg ("High Salzburg Fortress") was built, and further expanded over time.

During Mozart's era, Salzburg was part of the Holy Roman Empire. After the *Anschluss* - the German occupation and annexation of Austria on March 12, 1938 - Salzburg was annexed to Hitler's Third Reich. German troops stormed the city, and political opponents, Jewish citizens, as well as other minorities were arrested and deported. The historic Jewish synagogue was also destroyed at this time. American troops entered Salzburg on May 5, 1945, and the city became the center of U.S.-occupied territory after World War II, until Austria was finally declared independent in 1955.

Salzburg was also the birthplace of renowned 18th-century composer Wolfgang Amadeus Mozart. When we arrived, the city was in the middle of the *Salzburger Festspiele* ("Salzburg Festival"), an annual event held each summer, featuring preeminent music and drama productions. The *Festspiele* was originally established in 1920 and rose to prominence as the premier summer opera festival, especially for works by Mozart. In 1936, the festival featured a performance by the Trapp Family Singers, whose story was dramatized in the world-famous musical and film *The Sound of Music.*

The festival's popularity suffered a major decline after the Anschluss, when conductors and performers were dropped or resigned in protest, and Jewish artists were forced to emigrate. In 1944, it was cancelled altogether by the order of Reich Minister Joseph Goebbels. However, in the summer of 1945, the *Salzburger Festspiele* was immediately reopened after the Allied victory in Europe near the end of World War II. In 2006, Salzburg celebrated the 250th anniversary of Mozart's birth by staging all 22 of his operatic compositions! I would have loved to take

Figure 87. Mozart's Geburtshaus on Getreidegasse 9, Salzburg.

Alexis to one of these performances, but when I learned that each ticket would cost $350 per person, I had to regretfully decline, as we simply could not afford such luxuries.

We visited Mozart's birthplace on Getreidegasse 9, where he spent his early years with his family and composed his first musical pieces. The house was originally built in the 12th century, on part of a garden belonging to the Benedictine monks of St Peter's Abbey. In 1880, the house was turned into a museum, which features his *kindergeige*, or miniature children's violin, his harpsichord, original portraits, early editions of his music, as well as the clavichord on which he composed his famous Masonic opera, *The Magic Flute*. On the first floor,

Maria Rosa

Figure 88. Mozart's harpsichord.

one can view an historical replica of the living conditions in Mozart's day, with antique period furniture.

All around the city, we were presented with endless varieties of chocolate *Mozartkugel* ("Mozart ball"), a delicious candy created in 1890 by Salzburg confectioner Paul Fürst, and named after Mozart. Genuine Fürst confectionery shops still produce the original Salzburg Mozartkugeln by hand according to the original recipe and technique, but there are also numerous imitation products for sale, most of which are made using mass-market industrial methods and ingredients which were not in the original recipe.

The bonafide hand-made bonbon begins with a ball of green pistachio marzipan, covered in a layer of nougat. It is then placed on the end of a small wooden stick and dunked into dark chocolate to coat it, then allowed to cool and harden. Once the stick is removed, the remaining hole is filled with chocolate, and the ball is wrapped by hand in blue-silver tin foil. When Fürst presented his sweet creation at a Paris fair in 1905, he was awarded a gold medal. It is still an Austrian favorite even today, as millions of these flavorful treats are sold every year. Alexis of course insisted on bringing some home!

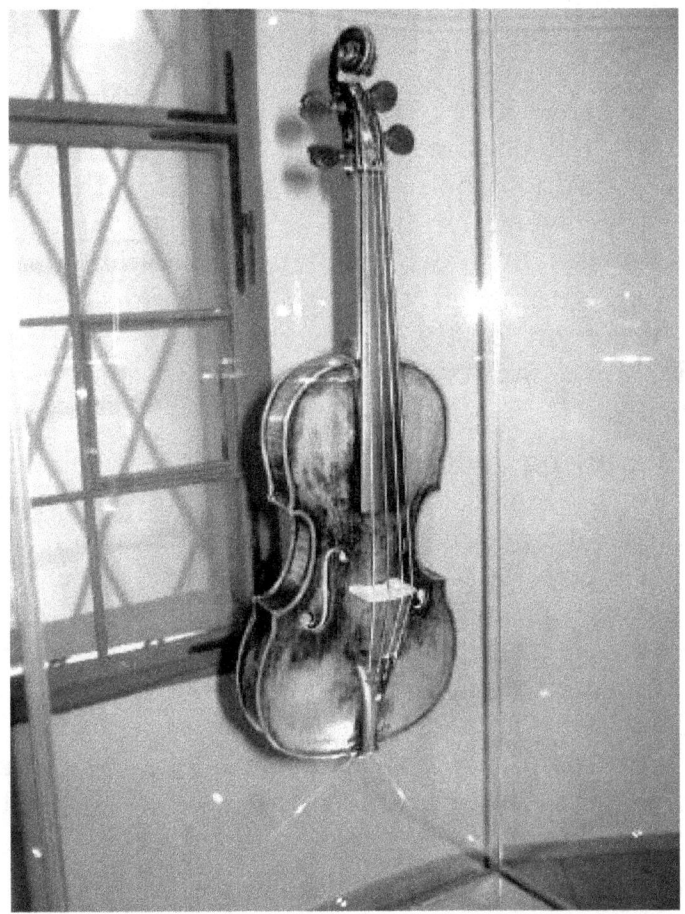

Figure 89. Mozart's *kindergeige*, or children's violin.

Eagle's Nest

The food at our Salzburg hotel was terrific, but our accommodations were otherwise terrible. There was no air conditioning. The bathroom faucet was leaking so much that the tap water ran onto the counter and down to the floor. The metal toilet seat covers dispenser fell off the wall and rattled to the ground with a booming crash. When I turned on the hanging lamp, the switch emitted scintillating sparks and blew out the bulb with a snap, crackle, and poof. When we attempted to close the window shutters, they broke off of their hinges. I was beginning to wonder if we had just rented the Halloween "House of Horrors."

While enjoying a lovely bowl of *Kasnocken* (cheese dumplings made with onions and "Pinzgauer Bierkäse," a special regional cheese marinated with beer), a fellow European tourist, introducing himself as Viktor, greeted me and struck up a lively conversation about our travels. He was fresh from a visit to Berchtesgaden in the German state of Bavaria, just over the Austrian border from Salzburg. This picturesque region is situated in the Alps and renowned for its rocky mountain peaks, as well as a deep glacial lake called the Königssee.

Above the town of Berchtesgaden is a mountainside retreat called Obersalzberg, named after the area's rock salt deposits. The scenic landscape grabbed Hitler's attention in 1923, when he learned about it just before his imprisonment at Landsberg Prison, after being convicted of treason. Following his release, in 1925 he stayed at a small cabin on the Obersalzberg, where he dictated the second part of his infamous book *Mein Kampf,* which earned him

To Hell and Back

Figure 90. *Kasnocken* (cheese dumplings with onions).

large royalties. As such, this cottage came to be called the Kampfhäusl.

By 1928, Hitler grew so fond of the area that he was using his royalty income to rent, and later buy, a mountain retreat called Haus Wachenfeld, which became the basis for a major political expansion. The region of Obersalzburg was purchased by the Nazis for the enjoyment of their senior leaders, turning the out-of-the-way retreat into a huge complex of Nazi buildings, most of which were closed to the public.

After Hitler's appointment as Chancellor of Germany in 1933, Berchtesgaden served as an outpost of the German *Reichskanzlei* (Imperial Chancellery) office, which caused it to become a strategic objective for Allied forces during World War II. Hitler renovated his mountainside chalet, transforming it into a sprawling residence known as the *Berghof*.

In the town below, the Nazis bought and renovated

Figure 91. The *Kelsteinhaus*, or Eagle's Nest.

the Berchtesgadener Hof Hotel, where many famous visitors came to lodge, including Hitler's mistress Eva Braun, Nazi Propaganda Minister Joseph Goebbels, SS Commander and Reich Leader Heinrich Himmler, German Field Marshall Erwin Rommel, as well as British Prime Minister Neville Chamberlain.

Viktor told me of the breathtaking view from the *Kelsteinhaus*, popularly nicknamed the "Eagle's Nest," which was built as a 50th birthday present for Hitler in 1939, as an extension of the Obersalzberg complex in the mountains above Berchtesgaden. This chalet sits on a 6, 000-foot-high subpeak of the Kehlstein mountain and is still open to visitors today.

The Eagle's Nest can only be reached via a 4-mile-long road which cost the equivalent of 150 million Euros to build. It was considered a major engineering feat, as it features five tunnels during its 2,600-foot climb, but only one hairpin turn. The last 407 feet up to the Kehlsteinhaus are reached by an elevator whose shaft was bored straight down through the mountain and linked to a tunnel through the granite below. The interior of the elevator is surfaced with green leather, polished brass, and Venetian mirrors.

The main reception room of the house itself features a striking stone fireplace made from red Italian marble, presented by Italian dictator Benito Mussolini. The Eagle's Nest was meant to serve as a retreat and a place to entertain foreign dignitaries on their visits, but Hitler rarely stayed at the property, even though he lived close by at the Berghof.

Viktor paused for a moment to order us both a plate of Salzburger Nockerl – sweet puffy dessert dumplings made with flour, egg, sugar, and vanilla, and served warm with powdered sugar or raspberry sauce. Between thirsty sips of beer and big bites of the Salzburg specialty soufflé, my talkative friend continued to narrate what he had learned.

Figure 92. Salzburger Nockerl, a dessert souffle.

The Eagle's Nest became a planned target for destruction by an Allied Forces air raid on April 25, 1945, but the small lodge on the edge of a looming cliff proved so elusive that Hitler's Berghof was targeted and heavily damaged instead. The remains of the Berghof were set on fire by retreating SS troops and plundered by locals after the arrival of Allied troops to the area on May 4, 1945.

After the war, Obersalzberg became a military zone and most of its former Nazi buildings were requisitioned by the US Army. The area was used for decades by the American military as a holiday retreat and recreation park. The Berghof ruins were demolished in 1953, and the Hof Hotel was demolished in 2006; the Kelhsteinhaus however survived mostly intact, being occupied as a military command post until it was handed back to the State of Bavaria in 1960.

Allied soldiers chipped off pieces from Mussolini's red marble fireplace as souvenirs to take home, and scrawled graffiti on the interior woodwork, which is still visible today. At the foot of the hill, an information center was constructed to remind visitors about Hitler and his Nazi regime. The Eagle's Nest itself became a restaurant, owned by a charitable trust, where Hitler's private study is now used as a storeroom for the cafeteria. The restaurant remains a popular and historically significant tourist attraction, featuring an indoor dining area and an outdoor beer garden with spectacular views. Viktor hoped to return again someday.

Figure 93. Mussolini's red marble fireplace at the Eagle's Nest.

Figure 94. The Festung Hohensalzburg (High Salzburg Fortress).

The Dungeon

With his belly full and his confidence high, Viktor asserted that I "absolutely must" take my family to visit Salzburg's very own mountaintop "eagle's nest," the *Festung Hohensalzburg* (High Salzburg Fortress). He even offered to show us around, so the next morning, Viktor, Jeanette, Alexis, and I jumped onto the cable rail leading up from the base of the large hill to the imposing fortress which overlooks the city of Mozart.

The steep cone-shaped rock outcrop, sitting on the northern edge of the Alps, had already been considered a point of strategic importance for centuries before the mountain became home to the iconic fortress. First built in 1077 at the behest of Archbishop Gebhard I, the Hohensalzburg Castle is surrounded by medieval stone walls and is one of the largest remaining 11th century castle complexes in all of Europe, measuring 820 x 490 feet, or over 9 acres.

The fortifications were constructed in three phases, to protect the prince bishops and their principality from attack after a dispute between German Emperor Heinrich IV and Pope Gregory VII, who was supported by the Archbishopric of Salzburg. Further improvements and fortifications were added over the centuries in response to the development of more powerful weapons technology with greater range.

At the top of the hill, we emerged into the spacious courtyard, with its ancient Linden or Tilia trees which seemed to have a personality of their own. Viktor took us first through a couple of lantern-lit medieval rooms, including a reconstruction of the stone-paved banquet hall with its wooden tables and benches,

To Hell and Back

Figure 95. Medieval dining hall at the Festung Hohensalzburg.

and a young maiden in period work clothes cleaning the floor, wooden bucket beside her. These soot-stained walls surely had many stories to tell about the everyday lives of the people of yesteryear.

Then there was the dungeon and torture chamber, with its vast array of ghastly torture implements. In 1612, the deposed Archbishop Wolf Dietrich von Raitenau died here in prison. There was even a heavy iron chastity belt, intended for virgin girls, which could only be unlocked with a key. A chill overcame me and I shuddered to imagine what any of these unlucky people must have endured at the hands of their wardens!

The Archbishopric of Salzburg, after winning independence from Bavaria in the late 1300s, became both an independent prince-bishopric and a State of the Holy Roman Empire; the castle, meanwhile, served to demonstrate and symbolize the political

Figure 96. Grated dungeon window at the Festung Hohensalzburg.

authority and power held by the prince bishops, who expanded the castle to protect their interests.

We then ascended the Reckturm watchtower, built in 1462, to enjoy the stunning 360° panoramic view. This observation tower is the best vantage point from which to view the entire city of Salzburg and the Alps to the south. The Krautturm or Pulverturm ("Gunpowder Tower") houses a large mechanical pipe organ, built in 1502, called the *Salzburger Stier* ("Salzburg Bull"). This antique organ is still played three times a day on special religious occasions.

Viktor took us back through the courtyard, with its idyllic surroundings, and onward to the next wing of the castle. He brought us to the illuminated chapel of Archbishop Leonhard von Keutschach, built in the early 1500s. This Catholic shrine is richly decorated, with a vaulted ceiling and many pieces of religious artwork.

Located in the upper floors of the fortress are the Prince-Bishop's apartments, with their magnificent State Rooms or regency suites. These were the highlight of our tour, due to their sheer decorative splendor and exquisite wealth. They are widely recognized as being some of the most beautiful Gothic secular chambers in Europe. The ceilings of these rooms are coffered and richly adorned with gold buttons, symbolizing the stars shining in the vault of heaven. A 17-meter-long supporting beam displays the coat of arms of Bishop Keutschach along with those of the Holy Roman Empire and the most powerful German towns and bishoprics connected with Salzburg at the time.

The walls of the Golden Chamber are decorated with golden vines, grapes, rosettes, and animals. The lower part of the wall also used to be covered with gold-embossed leather and velvet tapestry, which has

Figure 97. Walls and ceiling of the Golden Chamber, Festung Hohensalzburg.

now eroded away. In the corner sits a grandiose ceramic tiled stove, which served to heat the fortress apartments. The door conceals a toilet – a hole in the floor with a wooden frame – that was accessible from each story. Such accommodations were then considered state-of-the-art sanitary facilities!

Keutschach's bedchamber also features the coat of arms of Salzburg, as well as that of Keutschach himself, which comically includes his unique turnip symbol in its shield design. One can rest assured that this lavish Archbishop wasn't picking any turnips himself! In fact, he became rather infamous, as he expelled the Jews from Salzburg in 1498 and had their synagogues destroyed. Perhaps in remembrance of such events, a bitter joke still circulates among some Austrian folk to this day, shortening his name to Baron von Kuhscheiss - "Lord of Cow Manure."

Despite its notoriety, the fortress never faced a full-blown military attack. The only time it actually came under siege was during the German Peasants' War of

1525, when a group of farmers, miners, and townspeople attempted to oust Keutschach's successor, but failed to take the castle.

In 1813, the state of Salzburg was secularized and assimilated into the country of Germany. During the 19th century, the Hohensalzburg fortress was used as a barracks, storage depot, and dungeon before being abandoned by the military in 1861. It was then refurbished in the late 19th century onwards, and became a major tourist attraction after the Festungsbahn cable car was opened in 1892.

During the early 20th century, the dungeon was once again used as a prison, holding Italian POWs during World War I. Rumor has it that unwelcome Nazi activists were also thrown into the dungeon before the *Anschluss* in the 1930s.

The fortress museum displays Salzburg's military history from the 11th century up to the 21st century, including weaponry, uniforms, and other military artifacts. The Rainer Regiment Museum features a memorial plaque for members of the Archduke Rainer

Figure 98. Golden Chamber in the Fortress Hohensalzburg.

Infantry Regiment who died during World War I. Another permanent exhibit displays weapons and medals used by the Austrian army during World War I, as well as World War II photos of various Nazi officers in uniform. The Austrian Army developed a defense plan in 1938 against Nazi Germany, but politics prevented it from being implemented.

The castle also includes a small but fun interactive marionette museum. There is even a photo opportunity wherein you can stick your face into puppet cutouts, or cast yourself as a puppet from the *Sound of Music.* Numerous concerts, musical performances, and medieval festivals are held at the fortress on select days of the year, contributing to a sophisticated and refined atmosphere.

The Festung Hohensalzburg stands today as one of the best preserved castles in Europe and remains a popular destination for tourists - and as Viktor emphasized, a must-see for every visitor to Salzburg.

Figure 99. Festung Hohensalzburg.

Cathedral of the Saints

Viktor was due to depart for his next destination, so he bid us a warm farewell as we settled back into our shoddy hotel room, hoping another random fixture wasn't about to come crashing down at any minute. We decided the next morning to visit the iconic Salzburg Cathedral, located right underneath the Hohensalzburg Castle.

This Roman Catholic cathedral was originally founded by Saint Vergilius of Salzburg in 774 atop the remnants of a Roman town, possibly using the foundations of an earlier church built by Saint Rupert. Ironically, the building burned down in 842 after being struck by lightning. As a result, the original church underwent at least three extensive building and renovation campaigns during the early Middle Ages, eventually taking the form of a Romanesque-style basilica.

It was again severely damaged in 1598, and after several failed restoration attempts, Prince-Bishop Wolf Dietrich Raitenau finally ordered the building to be demolished. Inspired by the contemporary Italian Baroque architecture he had seen in Rome, Archbishop Raitenau hired an Italian architect to draw up plans for a comprehensive new cathedral in the Baroque style, which was subsequently completed by his successors. After additional changes, the monumental house of worship reached its present form in the 17th century.

A modern excavation site under the cathedral, known as the *Domgrabungen*, allows visitors to view the basilica's foundation stones, as well as mosaics and other artifacts dating back to the time when the location was a forum in the ancient Roman city of

Maria Rosa

Figure 100. Facade of the Salzburg Cathedral.

Juvavum. The Salzburg Cathedral also contains a Gothic baptismal font, dating to the 14th century, in which composer Wolfgang Amadeus Mozart was baptized.

The body of the church is constructed from dark gray conglomerate stone, while the ornamentation and façade are made of bright marble from the Berchtesgaden Alps. The façade is richly decorated and framed by two towers; the north tower still houses an old oven used for baking communion bread. The front entryway houses three round arches or portals that provide access to three bronze doors. These portals are flanked by four large sculptures, depicting Saint Rupert holding a salt barrel, Saint Virgilius holding a church, Saint Peter holding keys, and Saint Paul grasping a sword. Atop the ledge above, on the central portion of the façade, stand figures of the four Biblical evangelists – Saints Matthew, Mark, Luke and John. At the very top of the façade is a statue representing the Transfiguration of Christ, flanked by Moses and the Prophet Elijah. Within the triune portals at ground level, the triple bronze doorways represent the three divine virtues of Faith, Hope, and Love.

The Salzburg Cathedral was damaged during World War II, when a bomb crashed through the central dome. Restoration work was finally completed in 1959. When one looks upward from the crossing below into the center of the dome, a depiction of the Holy Spirit in the form of a dove can be seen, emanating or surrounded by rays of gold.

Allied bombing greatly impacted Salzburg, destroying 7,600 homes and killing 550 residents. A total of 15 airstrikes destroyed 46% of the city's buildings, as well as its bridges. Nevertheless, much of Salzburg's antique Baroque architecture still survives intact, making it one of the few remaining European towns of this style.

American troops entered the city on May 5, 1945, and several displaced persons camps were set up there after the war, the majority of which provided shelter and basic care for inmates of Nazi concentration camps, labor camps, and prisoner-of-war camps that were freed by the Allied armies. Salzburg became the center of the American-occupied territory in Austria, and was eventually declared the capital city of the State of Salzburg.

Figure 101. Interior of the central dome, Salzburg Cathedral.

Gypsy Music and Garden Gnomes

A very short walk from the Salzburg Cathedral was the famous Mirabell Palace, with its bright, cheerful flower gardens, considered part of Salzburg's historic UNESCO World Heritage Site. Built at the behest of Prince-Archbishop Wolf Dietrich Raitenau in 1606, the Palace was intended as a residence for his mistress, Salome Alt. Over the years, fifteen children were born to them, ten of whom survived.

When Raitenau was deposed and arrested in 1612, Alt and her family were expelled. The Palace then received its current name of Mirabell, from Italian for "wonderful," "of wondrous beauty." It has since been rebuilt and redesigned twice, once after the building was damaged by the great fire that swept through Salzburg on April 30, 1818.

The palace's exquisite Marble Hall formerly served as the Archbishop's ballroom and a concert venue for composer Wolfgang Amadeus Mozart, as well as his father Leopold and sister Maria Anna, or "Nannerl." Today it is considered one of the most beautiful wedding halls in the world. Meetings, award ceremonies, and romantic "Salzburg Palace Concerts" are regularly held in the Marble Hall. However, the other rooms are not open to the public, as today they house the offices of Salzburg's mayor and the municipal council.

Adjacent to the palace are the eye-catching Mirabell Gardens, considered a horticultural and artistic masterpiece, with special attention paid to symmetry, balance, and color. The complex also features a "Hedge Theater" or sylvan theatre – a type of small outdoor auditorium situated in a green or wooded

Figure 102. Mirabell Palace and Gardens.

setting - created between 1704 and 1718. It is one of the oldest sylvan theaters north of the Alps.

We were sure we'd enjoy perusing the walkways among the intricately curved flower beds, rose bushes, bright green lawns, and manicured boxwood topiary hedges, all arranged in a neat and clean geometric layout. However, it was an unusually hot day in Salzburg. The sun was high in the sky, and the air was oppressive and stifling. Hordes of bees were collecting nectar from the open blooms and frequently crossing paths with curious tourists. Alexis ran in the opposite direction screaming, afraid the busily buzzing insects were surrounding her and would soon sting her. Perhaps we should have taken cover in the large orangerie or greenhouse conservatory, used in the 18th century as a winter home for the orange trees - and now open year round!

We stopped for a break at a small ice cream stand, hoping we would find a refreshing treat. I ordered a cone for each of us. What we received was very disappointing: cheap, plain vanilla mush, already soft and sloppy the moment it was served to us out of an unrefrigerated tub. In fact, we seemed to encounter similar refrigeration problems throughout the duration of our trip.

As we hurriedly licked our pathetic excuse for an ice cream cone before it would melt into a soggy puddle, we took a closer look at the many fine sculptures and fountains positioned throughout the garden, which were crafted by Austria's best known artisans,

Various mythological-themed statues date back to 1730, depicting the Ancient Greek and Roman Gods and Goddesses. Diana, Minerva, Venus, and Juno stand with the four seasons, represented by Flora (spring), Ceres (summer), Pomona (fall), and Vesta (winter). Statues of Apollo, Jupiter, Mercury, Vulcan, Mars, Kronos, Bacchus, and Hercules stand nearby.

Figure 103. Mirabell Gardens.

Figure 104. Pegasus fountain, where *The Sound of Music* was filmed.

Another octagonal fountain is surrounded by four marble statues, sculpted in 1690 by Ottavio Mosto. These symbolize the four classical Elements - Water (the abduction of Helen by Paris, which started the Trojan War), Fire (Aeneas fleeing from the flames of Troy with his father), Earth (the abduction and rape of Persephone, Zeus' daughter, by Pluto, Lord of the Underworld), and Air (the battle between Hercules and Antaeus). There is also a Pegasus fountain, installed in 1913.

Additionally, an eccentric Dwarf Garden features a number of misshapen creatures carved from Berchtesgaden marble. These funny little dancing gnomes looked like they were about to start walking off on their own!

The Mirabell Gardens were opened to the public by Emperor Franz Joseph in 1854. Several scenes from

The Sound of Music were filmed there. The movie and musical were based on the true story of Maria von Trapp, who became governess for an aristocratic family in Salzburg and fled the Nazi German Anschluss. Maria and the von Trapp children sang "Do-Re-Mi" while dancing around the Pegasus fountain, using the steps as a musical scale. Other scenes were also filmed in and around Salzburg, as well as in the Alps, where Maria sang and danced atop a flower-covered hill during her signature scene. As a result, the city draws many visitors who wish to visit these famous filming locations. The Mirabell Gardens also remain a popular backdrop for photographers and a favored location for weddings.

Hot and tired, we decided it was time to leave. But then, we heard the sounds of exotic music drifting on the air from a nearby square. Alexis ran to go take a look, and I followed after her. The sweet melodies were produced by a group of street musicians who appeared to be Romas or Romani people, popularly known as Gypsies. This distinct ethnic group originated in India during the Middle Ages, and are famous for their traditional semi-nomadic lifestyle (although many contemporary Romani are no longer nomadic). Their name derives from the old belief that the Roma originated in Egypt, with one narrative account saying they were exiled from Egypt as punishment for allegedly harboring the infant Jesus after Mary and Joseph fled Herod's Massacre of the Innocents.

The Romani endured centuries of persecution, which reached its height during World War II with the *Porajmos*, the genocide perpetrated by the Nazis during the Holocaust. Romas living in Nazi Germany were stripped of their citizenship in 1935, after which they were subjected to violence, imprisonment in concentration camps, and eventually genocide in extermination camps. This policy was extended to many areas occupied by the Nazis and their allies during the war. During Nazi reign, a so-called Roma "work education camp" was built in Salzburg, which provided slave labor to local industry, before deporting the workers to German ghettos or death camps. An estimated 500,000 to 1,000,000 Romani died in the Holocaust.

These modern-day Romas dancing in the square were considerably better off. They moved in a tight circle, performing beautiful songs on flutes, hand drums, acoustic guitars, and other portable instruments. The leader, playing the panpipes, pranced around like a veritable Pan! They were even selling cassette tapes with their recordings on nearby stands, as well as hand-crafted jewelry mementos. Obviously they had seen considerable success with their musical endeavors, as they were driving Rolls Royces with their caravan trailers hitched behind – a sort of modern-day version of their stereotypical horse-drawn covered "Gypsy wagons."

The Romas' musical legacy is not only that of proficient street performers: the style and performance practices of Romani musicians have influenced well-known classical European composers, such as Johannes Brahms and Franz Liszt, as well as bolero, jazz, and flamenco music that is still popular even today.

Figure 105. Mirabell Gardens.

The Truffles of Venus

We finally returned to our hotel, thirsty and exhausted. The heat just would not let up; even with the windows wide open, we could get no relief from the stifling temperatures, and the air seemed to be growing more humid by the minute. Suddenly we realized that a huge Alpine thunderstorm was moving in.

Outside our window, we could see several bolts of lightning hitting the nearby Alps in succession, followed by deafening thunderclaps. The electrical storm continued for hours, with the rain pouring down and the thunder roaring. It was quite frightening, as we were so close to the action, and the atmosphere seemed to buzz with nervous energy. At the same time, impoverished residents of a nearby apartment building across the street grew very loud and agitated. Some ran out into the street, screaming and hollering at others who were leaning out of their windows above; others went out onto their balconies and hung from the rails like grapes, as if they had some crazy death wish.

This terrible noise and commotion, added to the storm, continued until 3 o'clock in the morning. I had never experienced anything like this in my life! To make matters worse, Alexis was feeling sick and suffering from the unrelenting heat. She begged for an ice-cold soft drink. Looking inside our self-serve hotel mini fridge, one miniscule 6 oz. bottle of Coca-Cola was priced at $3.00 USD.

On our last day in Salzburg, Jeanette was determined to seek out the famous chocolate confection devoured by Mozart's wife Constanze in the Academy Award-winning film *Amadeus* (1984). *Capezzoli di Venere* are

Figure 106. The Truffles of Venus.

often called Truffles of Venus, but the direct translation from the Italian is "Nipples of Venus," due to their naughty appearance. Venus was the Roman Goddess of love, beauty, and fertility, and these sweet treats named after her also inspired Juliette Binoche to tempt the well-restrained and stoic Comte de Reynaud in the movie *Chocolat*.

"Venus Nipples" are quite different from Mozartkugel. These classic Italian truffles are created by dipping and rolling brandied chestnuts in a buttery dark chocolate ganache, then coated with creamy white chocolate that is allowed to cool and harden. Finally, they are topped off with a nipple of pale pink-colored white chocolate. These delicious desserts have a long history and may originate from the gourmet French kitchen of César, duc de Choiseul, comte du Plessis-Praslin, who was an ambassador to Italy (1602 -- 1675).

In the movie *Amadeus*, when Mozart's rival - jealous court composer Antonio Salieri - offered the rich truffles to Constanze, he encouraged her by saying, "They're Roman chestnuts in brandied sugar. Try one. Go on, try one!" When actress Elizabeth Berridge was filming this scene, she didn't know she would be allowed to spit out the candy (which were in reality only lumps of marzipan) between takes. As a result, she ended up eating about 15 whole pieces! Unfortunately, she later described how she thought they were disgusting, and that she eventually made herself sick. Jeanette and Alexis, however, savored them for days to come.

When we were ready to leave Austria and return to Los Angeles, I attempted to confirm my reservation, as we already had paid for our return tickets. But suddenly, I was told that we "had no tickets." I almost panicked in disbelief, knowing this could turn into a disaster as we were already running short of money.

I braved the crowds at the huge international airport, trying to find someone to talk to, but hardly anybody wanted to listen. Perhaps in response to some sort of international security alert, military personnel with AK-47 automatic rifles were standing guard next to staff and civilians. Anxious passengers were hovering at the counter with fistfuls of cash, apparently trying to bribe the clerks in order to obtain a ticket. This was unthinkable to me and I was already flat broke, as everywhere we went, restaurants, taxi drivers, and service people held out their hands, expecting a large tip.

Only when I started speaking in my native Austrian dialect did anyone pause to give me any consideration. Finally I was able to convey that we already had paid tickets, and we were eventually able to secure seats on the airliner. Had I not spoken and understood the local language, it is quite possible we would have never gotten back to Los Angeles without paying for another set of tickets.

This was the last trip we took to Europe, and I swore to myself never again. When we arrived at LAX, I kissed the ground, immensely grateful to be back home in the USA.

Figure 107. Entrance to the Ronald Reagan Presidential Library.

Figure 108. Air Force One Hangar, with Reagan's Presidential Motorcade.

The Ronald Reagan Presidential Library

On November 4, 1991, the Ronald Reagan Presidential Library was dedicated in Simi Valley, California, near Los Angeles. During the dedication ceremonies, five United States Presidents gathered together in the same place for the first time in history: Richard Nixon, Gerald Ford, Jimmy Carter, Ronald Reagan, and George H. W. Bush.

The Ronald Reagan Library, dedicated to the 40th President of the United States, was built entirely with private donations totaling $60 million. It functions as the repository for the presidential records of the Reagan administration, which include millions of documents, photographs, motion picture films, and audio tapes. The museum features a permanent exhibit of Reagan's life, as well as temporary exhibits under continuous rotation. Another prominent feature is a full-scale replica of the Oval Office.

I would visit the museum with Alexis when we were in the area, as she always enjoyed seeing the new exhibits and learning more about the historical events which marked Reagan's life and presidency. She was also in awe of the many beautiful and exquisite gifts on display from foreign leaders around the world, presented to President Reagan while he was in office.

The surrounding hilltop grounds feature an F-14 Tomcat supersonic fighter plane, a replica of a portion of the White House Lawn, expansive views, as well as a colorful piece of the Berlin Wall. The Berlin Wall was constructed by Soviet East Germany, starting August 13, 1961, and completely cut off West Berlin from East Berlin and East Germany.

Figure 109. Piece of Berlin Wall at the Reagan Library.

The communist Eastern Bloc, aligned with the Soviet Union, claimed that the wall was erected to protect them from "fascist" elements who wished to prevent the people of East Germany from building a socialist state. East Berliner authorities officially referred to the wall as the *Antifaschistischer Schutzwall*, or "Anti-Fascist Protection Rampart" – implying that West Germany had not yet been fully freed from Nazi influence. In actuality, millions had fled the communist Eastern Bloc during the decades following World War II, and the Berlin Wall now served to prevent further defection and emigration. The government of West Berlin condemned the wall's obstruction of freedom of movement, sometimes referring to it as the "Wall of Shame."

Along with the border which separated East Germany from West Germany, the Berlin Wall came to symbolize the "Iron Curtain" which separated democratic Western Europe from the Soviet Eastern Bloc during the Cold War.

On June 26, 1963, President John F. Kennedy visited West Berlin, speaking to an audience of 450,000 people. In his famous "Ich bin ein Berliner" speech, he declared the United States' support for West Germany and the people of West Berlin:

"Two thousand years ago, the proudest boast was civis romanus sum ['I am a Roman citizen']. Today, in the world of freedom, the proudest boast is 'Ich bin ein Berliner!'... All free men, wherever they may live, are citizens of Berlin, and therefore, as a free man, I take pride in the words 'Ich bin ein Berliner!'"

In another historic speech on June 12, 1987, President Ronald Reagan challenged Soviet General Secretary Mikhail Gorbachev to tear down the Berlin Wall as an indication of growing freedom in the Eastern Bloc:

"We welcome change and openness; for we believe that freedom and security go together, that the advance of human liberty can only strengthen the cause of world peace. There is one sign the Soviets can make that would be unmistakable, that would advance dramatically the cause of freedom and peace. General Secretary Gorbachev, if you seek peace, if you seek prosperity for the Soviet Union and eastern Europe, if you seek liberalization, come here to this gate. Mr. Gorbachev, open this gate. Mr. Gorbachev, tear down this wall!"

By 1989, Soviet power was beginning to erode, and a series of radical political changes helped to liberalize the Eastern Bloc. After several weeks of civil unrest, on November 9, 1989 the government of East Germany announced that all citizens could now visit West Berlin and West Germany. Celebrations ensued, with crowds of East Germans climbing onto and

Figure 110. Replica of President Reagan's Oval Office.

crossing over the Berlin Wall, joined by West Germans on the other side. Parts of the wall were chipped off and cut away as souvenirs over the following weeks. The remainder was eventually demolished with industrial equipment, paving the way for German reunification in 1990. The section of Berlin Wall on display outside the Reagan Library serves to commemorate these monumental events.

In 2005, the Reagan Library showcased a new and enormous permanent exhibit: the 90,000-square-foot Air Force One Pavilion, featuring the Boeing 707 aircraft flown by Air Force One during Reagan's administration. Boeing, the plane's manufacturer, disassembled the jet piece by piece for transport to the library. It was then reassembled and restored to museum quality, and raised on 25-foot-high pedestals within its own exhibit hangar. It is accompanied by a genuine presidential motorcade, including Reagan's 1984 parade limousine.

To Hell and Back

Figure 111. Piece of Berlin Wall at the Reagan Library.

When she visited, Alexis particularly enjoyed the library's annual holiday exhibits, especially "Christmas Around the World," featuring lavishly decorated and lighted Christmas trees, representative of the unique culture of each nation. She was also fond of the gift shop and their bags of jelly beans – Ronald Reagan's favorite snack. In fact, Reagan liked them so much that he kept a jar of jelly beans on his desk in the Oval Office, as well as on Air Force One in a special turbulence-proof container. He even sent them up into space on the Shuttle Challenger as a surprise for the astronauts! A portrait of President Reagan, made from 10,000 jelly beans, hangs in the presidential library. Another temporary exhibit, entitled "Nancy Reagan: A First Lady's Style," featured over 80 designer dresses belonging to the former First Lady.

The library has since become President Reagan's final resting place, and remains a fascinating and educational destination to visit year-round.

Maria Rosa

Figure 112. Christmas Trees at the Reagan Library.

Figure 113. Jewish Menorah exhibit at the Reagan Library.

The Northridge Earthquake

The weather had been unusually warm and muggy, almost tropical, in the middle of winter no less – a phenomenon which Southern Californians eventually termed "earthquake weather" or "shake 'n' bake." Then, on January 17, 1994, the Northridge earthquake struck.

It was 4:31 am, and a previously undiscovered blind thrust fault ruptured underneath the San Fernando Valley region of Los Angeles. Hitting almost the exact same area as the previously mentioned 1971 Sylmar Earthquake, this magnitude 6.7 quake produced approximately 20 seconds of extreme shaking and jolting. I woke up with a start to the sound of a deep rumble, almost a roar, as everything around me began to rattle and roll.

As I bolted out of my bedroom in this early morning hour, the ground seemed to push up beneath me one second, and then collapse below me the next, as if I were briefly walking on air - only to be thrown down and tossed upward again like a trampoline. This was no illusion: scientists later determined that the quake's ground acceleration was one of the highest ever recorded in an urban area in North America.

Alexis ran toward me, narrowly escaping a falling metal hat rack which slammed into the wall with a thud. All around the house, glass was breaking, décor was flying, and cabinets and bookshelves were falling forward to the ground, smashing anything left within them. Then everything went pitch black – the shaking had evidently knocked out the electricity.

I had never experienced such a strong earthquake before in my life; it was an extremely frightening event for me and my family. As soon as the ground

Figure 114. Collapsed freeway overpass after the 1994 Northridge Earthquake.

movement tapered off, I groped around in the dark by touch and memory, searching for a flashlight, only to be shaken once again by a magnitude 6.0 aftershock.

The initial earthquake had been felt as far away as Las Vegas, Nevada, and several thousand aftershocks hit in the following days and weeks. The immediate damage was quite severe. The TV had rolled onto the carpet, and now rested upside down with its cables ripped out; the refrigerator doors had swung open, with liquids spilling onto the kitchen floor; broken shards of glass and ceramic littered the ground everywhere.

Along with knocking out the electricity, the earthquake also knocked local radio and television stations off the air. Only after several hours were they able to come back online to cover the breaking news and devastation. In all, about 60 people had died and over 8,000 were injured. Many also suffered from stress-induced heart attacks and anxiety attacks over the following days.

As soon as the sun came up, around 7am that morning, I left the house, hoping to find an open supermarket where I could still buy a few supplies, including some water. Later that day, we were warned not to turn on the tap, as the earthquake had also interrupted the filtration systems at local water treatment plants, so the tap water was no longer safe to use.

I only found one grocery store that remained open. Hundreds of people were already milling around inside, grabbing up supplies as fast as they could; canned goods and packaged food had flown off the shelves and were now scattered all over the floor in heaps. Fresh produce was smashed or rolling around on wet, soiled mats. I literally had to walk through a disaster zone just to obtain a few basic items, which were selling out very quickly.

Figure 115. Gas fire and collapsed road after the 1994 Northridge Earthquake.

The earthquake caught worldwide attention due to the shocking damage done to Los Angeles' vast freeway networks. This included the Santa Monica Freeway or Interstate 10, which is known as the busiest freeway in the United States. Segments of other freeways also collapsed or split into pieces, causing congestion on nearby surface roads for months while repairs were underway.

In addition, the earthquake caused a tremendous amount of property damage, estimated at more than $20 billion and extending up to 85 miles away from the epicenter. Most notably, the Northridge Meadows apartment complex collapsed, killing sixteen people.

Eleven hospitals were damaged or unusable, and the scoreboard in Anaheim Stadium collapsed onto several hundred empty seats. Several universities were shut down, and California State University Northridge sustained heavy damage, including the collapse of parking structures. Several commercial buildings also collapsed, but loss of life was far less than it could have otherwise been, due to the Martin Luther King, Jr. holiday and the early morning hour at which the quake struck.

Over the following hours and days, further trouble became apparent: houses had shifted off their foundations, and unsecured water heaters tumbled down, causing gas lines to break and catch fire. Several underground water and gas lines were severed in the San Fernando Valley, resulting in simultaneous floods and fires on some streets. Water pressure dropped to nothing in some areas, making firefighting efforts very difficult. Landslides caused further damage and released airborne fungal spores into the atmosphere, resulting in an outbreak of Valley fever.

To Hell and Back

Our house was also in pretty bad shape – cracked walls, upended furniture, and irreplaceable knick-knacks broken into pieces that were impossible to repair. Periodic aftershocks shook our home and our nerves several times a day, and the general atmosphere in the city was downright eerie and frightening. Los Angeles Mayor Richard Riordan declared a state of emergency and issued curfews. Mail delivery was suspended for several days. Almost every business and public building was closed, including banks, post offices, and markets. Looking up at the multi-story structure where my daughter's office was located, I saw a huge crack running all the way down the side of the building, adjacent to where her desk would be sitting. Plaster was already beginning to warp and flake off. After another severe 6.0 aftershock that afternoon, we decided she had better move out at soon as possible.

California Governor Pete Wilson and President Bill Clinton visited Los Angeles to tour the earthquake-affected areas for disaster relief. A whole week passed before anything even began to return to normality. That daunting week will remain chiseled into my memory for as long as I live.

If there's one thing I'm extremely afraid of, it's earthquakes. I have trouble composing myself whenever they occur; I get soft and shaky in the knees every time, as in many ways the phenomenon reminds me of certain things I experienced during the war, back when I was a child in Austria. The shaking, rattling, and often destructive aftermath bring back very bad memories, especially of being bombed. So this is one thing I've never quite learned to cope with, no matter how long I've lived in California. But we're always reminded that we do reside in earthquake country, so we have to learn to live with that fact and be adequately prepared.

Often I have prayed that I will never have to go through a terrible experience like this again. Nevertheless, it is always wise to have an earthquake preparedness kit at the ready, with plenty of food, water and other supplies in case of an emergency. Better safe than sorry!

Figure 116. Gas fire and flood on the same street after the 1994 Northridge Earthquake.

Sour Melodies

During the following years, the entire family worked very hard to make progress, as well as to recoup the losses we suffered during the Northridge Earthquake. My daughter Jeanette managed a successful professional office, while my granddaughter Alexis, inspired by her love for Mozart, continued her piano studies. Now in high school, she also intended to study music in university.

We originally started her out very early with private piano lessons, beginning already in elementary school. Now, as she entered high school and made preparations for college, we needed to find a more professional teacher who would be able to prepare Alexis for her advanced university studies.

Soon, we were recommended to speak to a certain lady who was giving a classical piano concert in a senior home. Her playing sounded very proficient to us, so we asked her if she would teach Alexis on a private basis. She said, "Oh, I'm very busy right now. You'll have to wait a few weeks, but I'll let you know when I'm ready." We figured she was the right person, as she also had a grand piano in her studio, so we agreed to wait. Finally, she did contact us several weeks later, and Alexis commenced her studies with Mrs. A.

Mrs. A. recommended that we start out with lessons once a week for one hour. She demanded $30 per hour in advance – sometimes five or six weeks in advance. I thought her demands were rather excessive, but I believed it would be worth it for Alexis' sake. In spite of all this money I paid her, I was not permitted to enter her music room. Sometimes I was allowed to wait outside in the hallway; but most of the time, I was asked to sit outdoors in my car and wait, even if it was cold and raining. I thought this was rather unfriendly, and I often wondered why she behaved this way.

Eventually, my granddaughter and my neighbor, who also sent his two daughters to the same teacher, revealed some very "interesting" facts. Mrs. A did not allow the children to touch her grand piano, but made them play on a much smaller, cheaper instrument. Half of their lesson time each week was spent on things unrelated to playing piano, such as listening to records while reading along with the sheet music, rhythm exercises on drums and tambourines, as well as personal chit-chat. Meanwhile, Mrs. A. would often be busy in the kitchen stirring her crock pots, peeling potatoes, and washing dishes. She was currently going through a divorce and taking care of two teenaged kids (one of whom would often barge through the door unannounced before slamming it shut behind him) and she needed all the money she could get in order to hang onto her house. My neighbor told me he was unhappy with the progress his daughters were making, and was currently looking for a new teacher.

I decided to take a more active approach and observe for myself. I asked to be able to come inside her home studio to hear how my granddaughter was playing and such. Mrs. A obviously resented my request, but she didn't have much choice, since I insisted on it.

Three weeks were more than enough to disgust and convince me: one could not use her bathroom, as it was filthy and there was never any toilet paper. The toilet seat was always up and the door was open, so the housedog would frequently enter the bathroom to drink and slurp loudly out of the toilet bowl. The dog stank, and the entire house was dirty and unkempt. I pulled Alexis out immediately and looked for a new teacher.

We thought we would have better luck with the local community orchestra leader, who was also a trained classical pianist. Alexis had a piano at home, so Mr. B. would come to the house to teach. He asked her to join the orchestra, which sounded like a good offer - until we found out that he was married with two children while having an affair with the orchestra's first violinist! Friction was developing between him and his family, and we didn't think this would be a healthy environment for my granddaughter, so we let Mr. B. go as well.

The next teacher was recommended to us by a professor at the university Alexis would be attending in the future. Her house was some distance away, so there was quite a lot of travel time involved in seeing her each week. Mrs. C. was a talented pianist from a foreign country who also charged $30 per hour, as well as expecting occasional dinner invitations and holiday gifts from us. She had much knowledge to impart to Alexis, so it deeply irritated me to find out that she talked verbosely about her homeland and her private life during half of her lesson time. Is this what we drove for hours on the freeway for each week?

During Alexis' last summer vacation before entering university, Mrs. C gave her a poorly-written reference book about music composers. Rather than allowing Alexis to study at her own pace and enjoy her summer vacation, Mrs. C demanded that she finish reading the book from cover to cover before the fall semester began (even though, as an encyclopedic reference book, it was not intended for such). Alexis found the volume extremely boring and difficult, and felt that it completely ruined her summer vacation. Mrs. C. then surprised her with a pop quiz, just to make sure she had actually read it! Unfortunately, Alexis felt that the book did little to help prepare her for her university curriculum, and merely cast a dark cloud over the little bit of free time she had.

After her lesson one week, Mrs. C. insisted on taking Alexis and Jeanette down to a local pawn shop, which was owned by a friend of hers. Apparently, whenever she brought in customers who would buy some jewelry, she would receive a sales commission. Jeanette and Alexis bought nothing of course, as they were not able to splurge on frivolous luxuries, which infuriated Mrs. C. It became clear that she was mostly interested in seeing how much money she could squeeze from us. The relationship completely fell apart as a result, which suited us just fine, since we were tired of the long drive each week.

Alexis went off to university after that, and proudly graduated four years later as a Valedictorian!

Figure 117. Enjoy life and be happy!

Life's Lessons

What's kept me going all my life, despite the many challenges and disappointments, is my optimism and good sense of humor. And while we've all worked very hard to accomplish our goals, helping other people has always been high on our priority list. I still feel that the most valuable things in life truly are those which money cannot buy: love, family, kindness, and compassion.

My advice to my daughter, my granddaughter, and my readers is this: enjoy your freedom, your health, your friends and family, and your accomplishments; most importantly, remember to be thankful every day. Despite any troubles or difficulties, tomorrow is always a brand new day, with fresh opportunities, solutions, and surprises in store.

Freedom, peace of mind, a little comfort, the love of family, and a few good friends – that's all anybody ever needs. Don't forget to take a moment to relax and appreciate the beauty around you - enjoy the sunshine, the flowers, the trees, and your pets!

So be happy, and be good to each other!

- Maria

www.ingramcontent.com/pod-product-compliance
Lightning Source LLC
Chambersburg PA
CBHW050330170426
43200CB00009BA/1530